TAKE THREE

TAKE THREE

200 fabulous fuss-free recipes using three ingredients or less

Jenny White

HERMES HOUSE

This edition is published by Hermes House, an imprint of Anness Publishing Ltd,
Hermes House, 88–89, Blackfriars Road, London SE1 8HA; tel. 020 7401 2077; fax 020 7633 9499
www.hermeshouse.com; www.annesspublishing.com

If you like the images in this book and would like to investigate using them for publishing,
promotions or advertising, please visit our website www.practicalpictures.com for more information.

Publisher: Joanna Lorenz
Editorial Director: Judith Simons
Senior Editor: Susannah Blake
Copy-editors: Bridget Jones and Sally Somers
Photographer: Craig Robertson, with additional images by Gus Filgate
Home Economist: Jenny White
Home Economist's Assistant: Fergul Connolly
Stylist: Helen Trent
Designer: Paul Oakley
Additional Recipes: Joanna Farrow
Production Controller: Pedro Nelson

ETHICAL TRADING POLICY
At Anness Publishing we believe that business should be conducted in an ethical and ecologically
sustainable way, with respect for the environment and a proper regard to the replacement of the
natural resources we employ.
As a publisher, we use a lot of wood pulp to make high-quality paper for printing, and that wood
commonly comes from spruce trees. We are therefore currently growing more than 750,000 trees in
three Scottish forest plantations: Berrymoss (130 hectares/320 acres), West Touxhill (125
hectares/305 acres) and Deveron Forest (75 hectares/185 acres). The forests we manage contain
more than 3.5 times the number of trees employed each year in making paper for the books we
manufacture.
Because of this ongoing ecological investment programme, you, as our customer, can have the
pleasure and reassurance of knowing that a tree is being cultivated on your behalf to naturally
replace the materials used to make the book you are holding.
Our forestry programme is run in accordance with the UK Woodland Assurance Scheme (UKWAS)
and will be certified by the internationally recognized Forest Stewardship Council (FSC). The FSC is a
non-government organization dedicated to promoting responsible management of the world's
forests. Certification ensures forests are managed in an environmentally sustainable and socially
responsible way. For further information about this scheme, go to www.annesspublishing.com/trees

Previously published as *The Three Ingredient Cookbook*

NOTES
Bracketed terms are intended for American readers.
For all recipes, quantities are given in both metric and imperial measures and, where appropriate,
in standard cups and spoons.
Follow one set of measures, but not a mixture, because they are not interchangeable.
Standard spoon and cup measures are level. 1 tsp = 5ml, 1 tbsp = 15ml, 1 cup = 250ml/8fl oz.
Australian standard tablespoons are 20ml. Australian readers should use 3 tsp in place of 1 tbsp
for measuring small quantities.
American pints are 16fl oz/2 cups. American readers should use 20fl oz/2.5 cups in place of 1 pint
when measuring liquids.
Electric oven temperatures in this book are for conventional ovens. When using a fan oven,
the temperature will probably need to be reduced by about 10–20°C/20–40°F.
Since ovens vary, you should check with your manufacturer's instruction book for guidance.
Medium (US large) eggs are used unless otherwise stated.
Front cover shows *Noodles with Sesame-roasted Spring Onions* – for recipe, see page 163.

PUBLISHER'S NOTE
Although the advice and information in this book are believed to be accurate and true at the time of
going to press, neither the authors nor the publisher can accept any legal responsibility or liability for
any errors or omissions that may have been made nor for any inaccuracies nor for any loss, harm or
injury that comes about from following instructions or advice in this book.

Contents

Cooking with Three Ingredients

Just because a dish includes only a few ingredients, it doesn't mean you need to compromise on taste and enjoyment. Reducing the number of ingredients you use in a dish has many benefits. Not only does it make shopping easier and quicker, it also means spending less time on preparation because there's less measuring, peeling, scrubbing and chopping to be done. It also allows you to really enjoy the flavours of the few ingredients used. Fresh food tastes fantastic, so why not let the flavours of a few truly fabulous ingredients shine through rather than masking them with the taste of other ingredients?

Keeping it quick, keeping it simple

In today's busy world, time is of the essence – and no one ever seems to have enough of it. When you're trying to cram as much as possible into a single day, often the first thing that falls by the wayside is cooking. When you're busy, the last thing you feel like doing is spending an hour in the supermarket shopping for ingredients, then going home and preparing them before finally cooking a meal. The temptation is to grab a ready-prepared meal to heat up when you get home, or to pick up a takeaway – but sometimes, when you've had a hectic day at work or your kids have been running you ragged, what you really want is to sit down and relax with a tasty home-cooked meal. This book is devoted to helping you do just this.

The idea of making a dish that requires a huge list of ingredients can often put you off before you've even started – the shopping and preparation alone seeming like an unmanageable task. But the good news is that cooking doesn't need to be this way. It's incredibly easy to make delicious dishes using just a few simple ingredients – but the key to success lies in the ingredients you choose, and how you prepare and cook them.

Above and opposite: You need only three ingredients to make this fabulous dish of spaghetti with broccoli and spicy chilli. It tastes delicious and can be made in less than 15 minutes.

Using the right ingredients

The recipes in this book combine basic ingredients such as fruit, vegetables, meat, fish, herbs and spices, but they also make good use of ready-made or pre-prepared products such as curry pastes and pastry. Using these convenient products is a great way to save time, both on preparation and shopping, and can sometimes enhance the final dish in a way that the home-made version may not. For example, puff pastry is enormously difficult to make, while the bought varieties are easy to use, give great results and taste delicious.

When buying basic ingredients, always try to buy the freshest, best quality ones you can to get the maximum flavour. Really fresh ingredients also have the benefit of having a higher nutritional content. If you can buy organic produce, do so. The flavour will be better and you will have the knowledge that they do not contain chemical fertilizers and pesticides.

It is also a good idea to buy fruits and vegetables when they're in season. Although most are available all year round, you can really notice the difference between those that have been ripened naturally and those that have been grown out of season. Strawberries may be available in the middle of winter, but when you cut them open they are often white inside with a slightly waxy texture and none of the sweet, juicy, almost perfumed flavour of the summer fruits. There are so many fabulous ingredients at their peak in their own season that you don't have to buy unseasonal ones. Why buy tired-looking asparagus in autumn when there are plenty of mushrooms, squashes and root vegetables around – all of which can be made into a huge number of delicious, varied meals.

When buying pre-prepared or ready-made ingredients such as stocks for soups or custard to make ice cream, try to buy really good-quality, fresh varieties. When an ingredient is playing an intregral part in a dish, it needs to be well flavoured with a good texture and consistency. If you use a less good product with an inferior flavour, it will really show in the final dish. The same is true of flavouring ingredients such as curry pastes and spicy sauces – go for quality every time and you will reap the benefits.

About this book

Whether you're an experienced cook or an absolute beginner, you'll find the recipes in this book will suit you perfectly. There are dishes for every occasion: juices to quench your thirst; healthy breakfasts; midday meals; and simple suppers to make when time is short. There are also fabulous dishes to cook when you have more time on your hands or if you're entertaining guests. There is a selection of perfect picnic foods and divine dishes to eat outside when the weather's hot and sunny, and when you need a sweet treat, there are two whole chapters devoted to cookies, cakes and sumptuous desserts. No matter what the occasion, how much time you have, how many people you need to feed, or what you're in the mood for – you are sure to find the perfect dish within these pages.

Every recipe has an ingredients list of three items or fewer, and the only other things you will need will come from the storecupboard (pantry): oil or butter to cook with and salt and freshly ground black pepper to season the food. In some cases flavoured oils such as garlic-, lemon-, or herb-infused olive oil are used for cooking or drizzling, so it's well worth keeping a small selection of these oils in the storecupboard.

The Minimalist Kitchen

WHEN YOU'RE USING ONLY THREE INGREDIENTS OR
FEWER TO MAKE A DISH, EACH ONE NEEDS TO BE A
STAR PLAYER. THIS CHAPTER GUIDES YOU THROUGH
THE INTRICACIES OF CHOOSING, PREPARING AND
COOKING INGREDIENTS TO ACHIEVE THE BEST RESULTS
AND OFFERS TIPS ON MAXIMIZING FLAVOUR USING
SIMPLE COOKING TECHNIQUES. THERE ARE RECIPES
FOR MAKING BASIC INGREDIENTS SUCH AS FLAVOURED
OILS, STOCKS AND SAUCES, PLUS SUGGESTIONS FOR
SIMPLE ACCOMPANIMENTS AS WELL AS ADVICE ON
MENU PLANNING TO ENSURE SUCCESS EVERY TIME.

Equipment

You don't need a kitchen full of equipment to be a spontaneous and versatile cook. It is quality, not quantity, that counts when you're preparing and cooking food, particularly when choosing essential pieces of equipment such as pans and knives. As long as you look after them, these items should last for many years so are well worth the investment. The following section guides you through the essential items that make cooking as simple and enjoyable as possible, and also offers suggestions on how to improvise if you don't have the right piece of equipment.

Pans and bakeware

Always choose quality pans with a solid, heavy base because they retain heat better and are less likely to warp or buckle. Heatproof glass lids are useful because they allow you to check cooking progress without having to uncover the pan repeatedly.

Pans: small, medium and large When cooking large quantities of food, such as pasta or rice that need to be boiled in a large amount of water, the bigger the pan the better. It does not matter whether the pan is non-stick, but it is useful to have heatproof handles and lids so that the pan can double as a large ovenproof cookpot. A medium-size pan is ideal for cooking sauces and similar mixtures. Ideally, choose a non-stick pan, which will help to prevent thickened sauces sticking and burning. It also makes washing-up easier. The same guidelines apply to a small pan, which is ideal for small quantities.

Above: Choose good quality, heavy baking sheets because lightweight sheets tend to buckle in the oven.

Frying pan Select a non-stick pan that is shallow enough, so that you can easily slide a fish slice (metal spatula) into it. A pan with an ovenproof handle and lid can be placed in the oven and used as a shallow casserole dish.

Baking sheets Having one or two non-stick baking sheets in the kitchen is invaluable. They can be used for a multitude of tasks such as baking cookies and bread, or they can be placed under full dishes in the oven to catch any drips if the mixture overflows.

Roasting pan A good, heavy roasting pan is essential for roasting large cuts of meat and vegetables. Choose a large pan; you will achieve better results if there is room for heat to circulate as the food cooks. Potatoes, for example, will not crisp well if they are crammed together in a small pan.

Left: It is wise to invest in three good quality pans of different sizes. Treat them with care and you will get maximum use from them.

Cutting and grinding

Chopping, slicing, cutting, peeling and grinding are all essential aspects of food preparation so it's important to have the right tools for the job.

Chopping board Essential in every kitchen, these may be made of wood or plastic. Wooden boards tend to be heavier and more stable, but they must be thoroughly scrubbed in hot soapy water and properly dried. Plastic boards are easier to clean and better for cutting meat, poultry and fish.

Knives: cook's, vegetable and serrated When buying knives, choose the best ones you can afford. They should feel comfortable in your hand, so try several different types and practise a cutting action before you buy. You will need three different knives. A cook's knife is a good multi-purpose knife. The blade is usually about 18cm/7in long, but you may find that you prefer a slightly longer or shorter blade. A vegetable knife is a small version of the cook's knife and is used for finer cutting. A large serrated knife is essential for slicing bread and ingredients such as tomatoes, which have a hard-to-cut skin compared to the soft flesh underneath.

Vegetable peelers These may have a fixed or swivel blade. Both types will make quick work of peeling vegetables and fruit, with less waste than a small knife.

Graters These come in various shapes and sizes. Box graters have several different cutting blades and are easy to handle. Microplane graters have razor-sharp blades that retain their sharp edges.

Left: The traditional box grater is solid, reliable and easy to handle – with several different grating blades.

Pepper mill Freshly ground black pepper is essential for seasoning. It is worth buying a good pepper mill with strong blades that will not blunt easily.

Measuring equipment

Accurate measuring equipment is essential, particularly when making breads and cakes, which need very precise quantities of ingredients.

Weighing scales These are good for measuring dry ingredients. Digital scales are the most accurate but balance scales that use weights or a sliding weight are also a good choice. Spring scales with a scoop and dial are not usually as precise.

Measuring cups Suitable for dry or liquid ingredients, these standard measures usually come in a set of separate cups for different fractions or portions of a full cup.

Measuring jug/pitcher This is essential for liquids. A heatproof glass jug is useful because it allows hot liquids to be measured and it is easy to check the quantity.

Measuring spoons Table cutlery varies in size, so a set of standard measuring spoons is extremely useful for measuring small quantities.

Below: A heatproof measuring jug and a set of measuring spoons are invaluable for measuring liquids and small quantities.

Looking after knives

Although it may seem like a contradiction, the sharper the knife, the safer it is to use. It takes far more effort to use a blunt knife and this often results in accidents. Try to get into the habit of sharpening your knives regularly because the blunter they become, the more difficult they are to use and the longer it will take to sharpen them. Always wash knives carefully after use and dry them thoroughly to prevent them from discolouring or rusting.

Mixing, rolling and draining

Bowls, spoons, whisks and strainers are all important kitchen items that you can rarely do without.

Mixing bowls You will need one large and one small bowl. Heatproof glass bowls are a good choice because they can be placed over a pan of simmering water to heat delicate sauces and to melt chocolate.

Wooden spoons Inexpensive and essential for stirring and beating, every kitchen should have two or three wooden spoons.

Metal slotted spoon This large spoon with draining holes is very useful for lifting food out of cooking liquid.

Fish slice/metal spatula This is invaluable for lifting delicate fish fillets and other foods out of a pan.

Rolling pin A heavy wooden or marble rolling pin is useful for rolling out pastry. If you don't have one, use a clean, dry, tall glass bottle (such as a wine bottle) instead.

Below: *No kitchen should be without a good selection of wooden cooking utensils for mixing and stirring.*

Electrical appliances

Although not always essential, these can speed up food preparation.

Food processor This fabulous invention can make life a lot easier. It is perfect for processing soft and hard foods and is more versatile than a blender, which is best suited to puréeing very soft foods or liquids.

Hand-held electric whisk A small, hand-held electric whisk or beater is very useful for making cakes, whipping cream and whisking egg whites. Choose an appliance with a powerful motor that will last.

Above: *Metal ballon whisks are great for beating out lumps from mixtures such as sauces.*

Balloon whisk A metal whisk is great for softly whipping cream and whisking sauces to a smooth consistency. Whisks are available in all shapes and sizes. Do not buy an enormous whisk that is difficult to use and will not fit into pans; mini-whisks are not essential – you can use a fork instead.

Sieve For sifting flour, icing (confectioners') sugar, cocoa and other dry ingredients, a stainless steel sieve is essential. It can also be used for straining small quantities of cooked vegetables, pasta and rice. Wash and dry a sieve well after use to prevent it becoming clogged and damp.

Colander Choose a free-standing metal colander with feet on the base. This will keep the base of the colander above the liquid that is being drained off. A free-standing design also has the advantage of leaving both hands free to empty heavy pans.

Below: *A food processor is good for chopping and blending.*

Extra equipment

As well as the essential items, some recipes require other items such as tart tins (pans) and cookie cutters. The following are some items you may find you need.

Cookie cutters These make quick work of cutting out pastry and cookie dough. Metal ones have a sharper cutting edge so are usually preferable to plastic ones. If you don't have cutters, you can use a knife and cut around a template, but this takes more time.

Above: *Cookie cutters come in all kinds of shapes and sizes.*

Pastry brush Made of bristle, with a wooden or plastic handle, this is useful for brushing food lightly with liquid – for example, brushing meat or fish with oil or marinade while grilling (broiling), or brushing pastry with beaten egg or milk.

Above: *A pastry brush is useful when baking or grilling.*

Cake tins/pans These may have loose bottoms or spring-clip sides to allow easy removal of the cake. Be sure to use the size specified in the recipe.

Muffin tins/pans These consist of six or twelve fairly deep cups in a tray. They can be used for baking muffins, cupcakes, buns, bread rolls and deep tartlets.

Tart or tartlet tins/pans Available with straight or fluted sides, these are not as deep as muffin tins (pans). They come in a variety of sizes, from individual containers to very large tins. They are useful for baking all kinds of sweet and savoury tarts. Loose-bottomed tins are best because the contents are easier to remove.

Skewers These are used for kebabs and other skewered foods. Metal skewers are reusable and practical if you cook over the barbecue frequently, or cook kebabs that need lengthy cooking. Bamboo skewers are disposable and useful for foods that cook quickly – soak them in cold water for 20 minutes before use to stop them burning.

Palette knife/metal spatula This large, flat, round-bladed, blunt knife is great for spreading icing and fillings on cakes, as well as lifting delicate biscuits (cookies) off baking sheets and flipping pancakes.

Griddle pan A good quality, heavy griddle pan is useful for cooking meat and fish. The pan should be very hot before food is placed on it and the surface of the food should be brushed with a little oil to prevent it from sticking, rather than adding oil to the pan.

Wok This traditional Asian pan is larger and deeper than a frying pan, often with a rounded base and curved sides.

Below: *The ridges in the griddle pan allow fat to drain away and create attractive markings on the surface of the food.*

Below: *Double- and single-handled woks are versatile and make a useful addition to any kitchen. They are great for stir-frying, deep-frying, steaming and braising.*

Minimalist Cooking Techniques

When cooking with a limited number of ingredients, the trick is to bring out the flavour of each one. The choice of cooking method is important because it can affect the flavour quite dramatically. Seasonings and aromatics are used to complement and bring out the flavours of the main ingredients, while marinating or macerating help to intensify the relationship between the basic ingredient and the condiments or seasoning. The result is a full, rich flavour.

Cooking methods to maximize flavour

How you cook food can make a real difference to the end result. For example, long-boiled vegetables become soggy and insipid, devoid of nutrients and flavour. In contrast, lightly steaming vegetables, baking fish wrapped in paper or foil parcels, and dry-frying spices are simple techniques that trap and enhance the natural flavour of the food. Some methods also add other flavours during cooking: for example, sprinkling smoking chips on a barbecue gives the food an extra smoky flavour.

Cooking on a barbecue Good-quality lumpwood charcoal will impart its characteristic smoky flavour to the food. A variety of natural or synthetic aromatics can also be added, including hickory, oak, mesquite or applewood chips; woody herbs, such as thyme or rosemary – just the stalks will do; or shells from almonds or walnuts. Soak nutshells in cold water for about 30 minutes before adding them to the barbecue to help them smoke.

Below: *Cooking vegetables, fish or meat over charcoal can help to give the food a wonderful, rich, smoky flavour.*

Above: *Roasting vegetables in the oven really helps to bring out their sweet flavour as the natural sugars caramelize.*

Roasting This is a good method for cooking meat, poultry, fish and vegetables. Long, slow roasting transforms sweet vegetables such as (bell) peppers and parsnips, bringing out a rich, caramelized flavour.

Grilling/broiling This method adds flavour by browning or charring the surface of the food. To achieve a good result the grill (broiler) must be preheated before cooking so that it is as hot as possible when the food is placed under the heat. Grilling is excellent for cheese, fish, poultry and lean meat, such as steak.

Dry-frying Frying with no fat or oil is a useful technique for certain ingredients. Fatty meats such as bacon and pancetta release fat as the meat cooks, providing fat in which to cook the meat and any other ingredients added to the pan. Dry-frying whole spices, such as coriander or cumin seeds, enhances their taste, taking the raw edge off their flavour while making it more intense and rounded. This technique is also known as roasting.

Shallow frying Meat, poultry, fish and vegetables are all delicious pan-fried with a little oil or butter. They can be cooked quickly over a high heat to seal in the flavours, or slowly over a low heat to achieve tender, juicy results.

Deep-frying Meat, poultry, fish, vegetables and even fruit are delicious cooked in hot oil. It is a very quick method and gives rich results. The outside of the food is sealed almost as soon as it hits the oil, forming a crisp exterior that encloses the flavour and juices of the ingredients. Most foods need to be dipped in a protective coating such as batter or breadcrumbs before frying.

Steaming This healthy cooking method is excellent for quick-cooking foods such as vegetables and fish. The natural flavours and nutrients of the food are retained giving moist, tasty results. Few additional ingredients or flavourings are needed when steaming.

Above: *Deep-frying is a quick way of cooking that produces richly flavoured food with a crisp yet succulent texture.*

Below: *Steaming is a delicate cooking method that is perfect for foods such as dumplings, vegetables and fish.*

Microwaving Vegetables, such as peas and green beans, can be cooked successfully in a microwave. The result is similar to steaming, and traps all the flavour and nutrients. Before cooking, place the vegetables in a suitable covered container with a little added water, then cook on full power.

Baking in parcels Traditionally known as cooking *en papillote*, this cooking method is a form of steaming. It is perfectly suited to foods such as fish and vegetables. The food is wrapped in baking parchment or foil to make a neat parcel, then baked. The steam and juices from the food are trapped within the parcel as it cooks, capturing the full flavour. Be sure to fold or crumple the edges of the parcel well to ensure that all the steam and juices are retained.

Dry-frying whole spices

1 Heat a small frying pan over a medium heat and add the spices. Cook, stirring occasionally, until the spices give off their aroma – take care not to let them burn.

2 Tip the toasted spices into a mortar and roughly crush them with a pestle. (Dry-fry spices freshly, as and when you need them.)

Below: *Fish, such as salmon, is delicious wrapped in a paper parcel with simple flavourings, then baked in the oven.*

Simple ways of introducing flavour

As well as selecting the cooking method best suited to the ingredients, there are several quick and simple methods of adding flavour using herbs, spices and aromatics. Match the seasoning to the ingredient and go for simple techniques such as marinating, stuffing or coating with a dry spice rub, which will help to intensify the flavours.

Flavours for fish Classic aromatics used for flavouring fish and shellfish include lemon, lime, parsley, dill, fennel and bay leaves. These flavours all have a fresh, intense quality that complements the delicate taste of fish and shellfish without overpowering it. All work well added before, during or after cooking.

• To flavour whole fish, such as trout or mackerel, stuff a few lemon slices and some fresh parsley or basil into the body cavity before cooking. Season with plenty of salt and freshly ground black pepper, then wrap the fish in foil or baking parchment, ensuring the packet is well sealed. Place the fish in an ovenproof dish or on a baking tray and bake until cooked through.

• To marinate chunky fillets of fish, such as cod or salmon, arrange the fish fillets in a dish in a single layer. Drizzle the fish with olive oil, then sprinkle over a little crushed garlic and grated lime rind and squeeze over the lime juice. Cover the dish in clear film (plastic wrap) and leave to marinate in the refrigerator for at least 30 minutes. Grill (broil) lightly until just cooked through.

• To make an unusual, yet delicious, marinade for salmon, arrange the salmon fillets in a single layer in an overproof dish. Drizzle the fillets with a little light olive oil and add a split vanilla pod. Cover and marinate in the refrigerator for a couple of hours before cooking in the oven.

Pepping up meat and poultry Meat and poultry suit both delicate and punchy seasonings. Dry rubs, marinades and sticky glazes are all perfect ways to introduce flavour into the meat and poultry. Marinating the tougher cuts of meat, such as stewing steak, also helps to tenderize it.

• To make a fragrant Cajun spice rub for pork chops, steaks and chicken, mix together 5ml/1 tsp each of dried thyme, dried oregano, finely crushed black peppercorns, salt, crushed cumin seeds and hot paprika. Rub the Cajun spice mix into the raw meat or poultry, then cook over a barbecue or bake until cooked through.

• To marinate red meat, such as beef, lamb or venison, prepare a mixture of two-thirds red wine to one-third olive oil in a shallow non-metallic dish. Stir in some chopped garlic and bruised fresh rosemary sprigs. Add the meat and turn to coat it in the marinade. Cover and chill for at least 2 hours or overnight before cooking.

• To make a mild-spiced sticky mustard glaze for chicken, pork or red meat, mix 45ml/3 tbsp each of Dijon mustard, clear honey and Demerara sugar, 2.5ml/^{1}/$_2$ tsp chilli powder, 1.5ml/^{1}/$_4$ tsp ground cloves, and salt and freshly ground black pepper. Cook the poultry or meat over the barbecue or under the grill (broiler) and brush with the glaze about 10 minutes before the end of cooking time.

Below: *Brush on sticky glazes towards the end of cooking time; if the glaze is cooked for too long, it will burn.*

Above: *Adding a drizzle of sesame oil to stir-fried vegetables gives them a wonderfully rich, smoky, nutty flavour.*

Vibrant vegetables Most fresh vegetables have a subtle flavour that needs to be brought out and enhanced. When using delicate cooking methods such as steaming and stir-frying, go for light, fresh flavourings that will enhance the taste of the vegetables. When using more robust cooking methods, such as roasting, choose richer flavours such as garlic and spices.

• To make fragrant, Asian-style steamed vegetables, add a bruised stalk of lemon grass and/or a few kaffir lime leaves to the steaming water, then cook vegetables such as pak choi (bok choy) over the water until just tender. Alternatively, place the aromatics in the steamer under the vegetables and steam as before until just tender.

• To add a rich flavour to stir-fried vegetables, add a splash of sesame oil just before the end of cooking time. (Do not use more than about 5ml/1 tsp because sesame oil has a very strong flavour and can be overpowering.)

• To enhance the taste of naturally sweet vegetables, such as parsnips and carrots, glaze them with honey and mustard before roasting. Mix together 30ml/2 tbsp whole-grain mustard and 45ml/3 tbsp clear honey, and season with salt and ground black pepper. Brush the glaze over the prepared vegetables to coat completely, then roast until sweet and tender.

Fragrant rice and grains Classic accompaniments, such as rice and couscous, can be enhanced by the addition of simple flavourings. Adding herbs, spices and aromatics can help to perk up the rice and grains' subtle flavour. Choose flavourings that will complement the dish that the rice or grains will be served with.

• To make exotic fragrant rice to serve with Asian-style stir-fries and braised dishes, add a whole star anise or a few cardamom pods to a pan of rice before cooking. The rice will absorb the flavour during cooking.

• To make zesty herb rice or couscous, heat a little chopped fresh tarragon and grated lemon rind in olive oil or melted butter until warm, then drizzle the flavoured oil and herbs over freshly cooked rice or couscous.

• To make simple herb rice or couscous, fork plenty of chopped fresh parsley and chives through the cooked grains and drizzle over a little oil just before serving.

Below: *Snipping fresh chives into a bowl of couscous not only adds flavour, but also adds a decorative finish to the side dish.*

Fruit

Widely used in both sweet and savoury dishes, fruit can be used either as a main ingredient or as a flavouring to complement and enhance the taste of other ingredients. The many different varieties offer the cook ample opportunity to create fabulous dishes – whether it's cod fillets with a squeeze of lime juice, a stew of lamb and tangy apricots or a sumptuous dessert made with soft, juicy summer berries.

Orchard fruit

This family of fruit includes apples, pears and quinces, which, depending on the variety, are in season from early summer to late autumn (fall). Choose firm, unblemished fruit and store in a cool dry place.

Apples There are two main categories of apples – eating and cooking. Eating apples have sweet flesh and taste good raw. Many can also be used for cooking; they remain firm making them ideal for pan-frying and open tarts. Cooking apples have a tart flavour and are too sharp to eat raw. When cooked, their flesh tends to break down and become pulpy, making them ideal for sauces and purées.

Pears Most commercially available pears are dessert fruits, just as good for eating as for cooking. They can be pan-fried or used in tarts and pies. They are also excellent poached, especially in a wine syrup.

Quinces Related to the pear, quinces have hard, sour flesh. Cooking and sweetening brings out their delicious, scented flavour. They are worth buying when you find them, and are often used in jellies and sauces.

Stone fruit

Peaches, nectarines, plums, apricots and cherries all belong to this family of fruit, which contain a stone (pit) in the

Above: *Sweet, juicy peaches are delicious served fresh in salads or poached in wine.*

middle. Most stone fruits are at their best through the summer months but some, such as plums, are best through the autumn. Choose firm, smooth-skinned fruit without any blemishes and store in a cool, dry place, preferably the refrigerator. They are used raw or cooked. When eating raw, eat at room temperature.

Above: *Fresh raspberries are perfect for breakfast and dessert dishes.*

Soft fruit

These delicate fruits, which include strawberries, raspberries, blackberries, blackcurrants, redcurrants and white currants, need careful handling and storing. Choose brightly coloured fruit and check for signs of grey mould or overripe specimens. Store in the refrigerator for up to 2 days. They are rich in vitamin C.

Citrus fruit

Oranges, lemons, limes, grapefruit, mandarins and satsumas are popular citrus fruits; but there are also hybrids such as clementines. The lemon is probably the most versatile member of the citrus family, with many uses in both savoury and sweet cooking. Citrus fruits are available all year round, with satsumas and clementines at their best in winter. Choose plump fruit that feels heavy. The skin should be bright and not shrivelled. Most citrus fruit is coated with wax to prevent moisture loss, so buy unwaxed fruit when using the rind in a recipe, or scrub the fruit well before use.

Segmenting oranges

1 Cut a slice off the top and bottom of the orange to remove the peel and pith. Stand the fruit on a board and cut off the peel and pith, working around the orange in strips.

2 Hold the orange over a bowl to catch the juices. Cut through one side of a segment, between the flesh and membrane, then cut through the other side of the segment to remove the flesh. Continue removing the segments in this way, leaving behind the clutch of membranes.

Exotic fruit

Once expensive and rarely available, these wonderful fruits are now widely available in supermarkets throughout the year. Eat them fresh or use them in recipes.

Mangoes There are many varieties of this sweet, fragrant, juicy fruit, which are delicious eaten on their own with a squeeze of lime juice, or used in recipes. Choose mangoes that have a fragrant smell, even through the skin, and give slightly when gently squeezed. Store in a cool place, but not the refrigerator, for up to a week.

Pineapple These sweet, tangy, juicy fruits are delicious in fruit salads and desserts. When choosing a pineapple, pull off one of the green leaves at the top – if it comes away easily, the pineapple should be ripe. Store in a cool place, but not the refrigerator, for up to a week.

Kiwi fruit The pale green flesh of kiwi fruit is full of sweet-sharp flavour that goes well with other fruit in salads and is good in various desserts and savoury cooking. Kiwi fruit are rich in vitamin C. Choose fruit with smooth, plump skin and store in the refrigerator for up to 4 days.

Passion fruit These small round fruit have a tough, wrinkled purple-brown skin. A passion fruit should feel heavy if it is nice and juicy. Store in the refrigerator.

Below: *Perfectly ripe pineapples have sweet, tangy flesh with a crisp bite and wonderful fragrance that is quite irresistible.*

Above: *Watermelon has bright pink flesh and a light, delicate flavour that is sweet yet refreshing.*

Other fruit

There are a few fruits that are delicious and very versatile but that don't fit into any particular group.

Rhubarb Tart, pink rhubarb is used in pies, tarts, crumbles and mousses. The stalks are edible but the leaves are poisonous so should be removed before cooking. Rhubarb is available from early spring to mid-summer. Pale, finer-textured pink forced rhubarb is available in January. It has a good colour and flavour, and is considered the best. Choose crisp, firm stalks and store in the refrigerator.

Melons There are two types of melon – dessert melon and watermelon. Charentais, Ogen, cantaloupe, Galia and honeydew melon are all dessert melons, which are in season from summer to winter. Slice them, remove the seeds and enjoy their fragrant flesh. Watermelons have crisp, juicy flesh, studded with dark seeds. They are best served chilled, and are in season from summer to autumn.

Figs Fresh figs with their dense, sweet red flesh are still considered a luxury outside the areas where they are grown. They are delicious raw or cooked and can be used in savoury or sweet dishes. Available in summer, handle figs carefully and store in the refrigerator for up to 2 days.

Grapes At their best in late summer, there are many varieties of grape, but the seedless ones are popular. Grapes can be used in many ways – served on their own as an accompaniment to cheese; used in fruit salads; or combined with savoury ingredients in salads.

Vegetables

Used in salads and savoury dishes, vegetables are delicious served as the main ingredient in a side dish, or as a flavouring ingredient within a main dish. Take your time when choosing vegetables, selecting healthy-looking specimens that are in season for maximum flavour – you'll really notice the difference.

Root vegetables and potatoes
Grown underground, these vegetables include carrots, parsnips, beetroot and turnips and many varieties of potato. They are very versatile: good for roasting, boiling, steaming and deep-frying. Choose firm vegetables with unblemished skins; avoid withered specimens and green-tinged potatoes, or ones with shoots. Store in a cool, dark place for up to 2 weeks. Scrub well if cooking in their skins.

Cabbages, broccoli and cauliflower
Members of the brassica family, these vegetables are packed with nutrients and good served in many ways.

Cabbage Regardless of variety, cabbage has a distinctive flavour and can be steamed, stir-fried or boiled. The white and red varieties are tight-leafed and ideal for shredding, and can be enjoyed raw in salads such as coleslaw. Green cabbage can be loose or close-leafed, smooth or crinkly and is best cooked. Buy bright, fresh-looking specimens and store in the refrigerator for up to 10 days.

Above: *Fresh, leafy purple sprouting broccoli is delicious steamed, boiled or stir-fried.*

Broccoli With a delicious flavour and crisp texture, broccoli and purple sprouting broccoli can be boiled, steamed and stir-fried. Choose specimens with bright green heads and no sign of yellowing. Store in the refrigerator and use within 4–5 days.

Cauliflower Good cut into florets and served raw with dips, cauliflower can also be boiled or steamed, and is delicious coated in cheese sauce. To ensure even cooking, remove the hard central core, or cut into florets. Choose densely packed heads, avoiding specimens with any black spots, and store in the refrigerator where they will keep for 5–10 days.

Above: *Plump juicy tomatoes have a rich, sweet flavour and are tasty used in salads or cooked in stews and sauces.*

Vegetable fruits
Tomatoes, aubergines, peppers and chillies are actually fruit, although they are generally used as vegetables. They all have a robust flavour and lovely texture and are widely used in Mediterranean-style cooking.

Tomatoes There are numerous varieties of tomatoes, including cherry, plum and beefsteak. They are eaten raw or cooked. Choose plump, bright-red specimens, ideally on the vine, and store in the refrigerator for 5–8 days.

Aubergines/eggplant These can be fried, stewed, brushed with oil and grilled (broiled), or stuffed and baked. Choose firm, plump, smooth-skinned specimens and store in the refrigerator, where they will keep for 5–8 days.

Peppers/bell peppers These may be red, yellow, orange or green, with the green specimens having a fresher, less sweet flavour. Peppers can be grilled, roasted, fried and stewed. Choose firm, unblemished specimens and store in the refrigerator for 5–8 days.

Chillies There are many types of chilli, all with a different taste and heat. As a general rule, the bigger the chilli, the milder it is; green chillies tend to be hotter than red ones.

Leafy green vegetables

There is a wide selection of leafy greens available, which may be used raw in salads or cooked.

Salad leaves There are many different salad leaves, including many types of lettuce. They are delicate and need to be stored in the refrigerator, where most will keep for a few days. Prepare salad leaves at the last minute.

Spinach Tender young spinach leaves are tasty raw. Mature spinach leaves can be fried, boiled or steamed until just wilted; they overcook very easily. Store spinach in the refrigerator for 2–3 days, and wash well before use.

Leafy Asian vegetables Asian vegetables, such as pak choi (bok choy), can be used raw in salads or cooked. Prepare in the same way as cabbage or spinach.

The onion family

This family includes onions, shallots, spring onions (scallions), leeks and garlic. All can be used as flavouring ingredients or cooked on their own. Roasting produces a rich, sweet flavour. Choose firm, unblemished specimens. Store onions in a cool, dry place for up to 2 weeks; store leeks and spring onions in the refrigerator for 2–3 days.

Beans, peas and corn

These are good boiled or steamed and served as a side dish, or used in braised dishes and stir-fries.

Green beans Many varieties of green beans are available throughout the year. Choose firm, fresh-looking beans with a bright green colour; avoid yellowish ones. Store in the refrigerator, where they will keep for up to 5 days.

Above: *Fresh green peas are delightfully sweet and tender.*

Peas Fresh peas are generally only available in their pods in the summer. Only buy really fresh ones because their natural sugar content quickly turns to starch, giving them a mealy texture. Frozen peas are often better than fresh ones because they are frozen within a short time of picking and retain all their natural sweetness.

Above: *Butternut squash has bright orange flesh, a lovely sweet flavour and smooth texture. Roasting brings out its flavour.*

Corn Large corn cobs are good boiled and served with butter, while baby corn are better added to stir-fries. Buy only the freshest specimens when they are in season because stale vegetables can be starchy.

Squashes

These vegetables come in many different shapes and sizes and include courgettes (zucchini); butternut, acorn and spaghetti squashes; and pumpkins and marrows (large zucchini). With the exception of courgettes, all need peeling and seeding before use. They can be cut up and boiled or baked whole. Select smooth, unblemished vegetables with unbroken skin. Most squashes can be stored in a cool place for 1 week, although courgettes should be stored in the refrigerator for 4–5 days.

Mushrooms

Freshly picked mushrooms have a rich, earthy flavour, but are rarely available to most cooks. Chestnut mushrooms are a good alternative; they have more flavour than cultivated mushrooms. Shiitake mushrooms are full-flavoured and delicious in Chinese- and Asian-style dishes.

There are many types of edible wild fungi or mushrooms of different flavours and textures. They tend to have a more intense flavour than cultivated mushrooms and are also more expensive and more difficult to find. Wild mushrooms are seasonal and can generally be found in late summer, autumn (fall) and winter. Choose firm, fleshy specimens and store them in paper bags in a cool place.

Dairy Produce

Milk and milk products, such as yogurt, milk and cheese, are widely used in cooking and can add a delicious richness to many sweet and savoury dishes. Strong-tasting cheeses, such as Gorgonzola or Parmesan, not only contribute a wonderful texture, but also add real bite to many savoury dishes.

Milk, cream and yogurt

These products are widely used in both sweet and savoury dishes, adding a rich, creamy taste and texture.

Milk Full-fat (whole) milk and lower-fat semi-skimmed and skimmed milk is pasteurised and available fresh or in long-life cartons. Buttermilk is a by-product of the butter-making process and is often used in baking.

Cream There are many different types of cream. Double (heavy) cream has a high fat content and can be poured, whipped and heated without curdling. Whipping cream has a lower fat content and can be whipped to give a lighter, less firm texture. Single (light) cream has a lower fat content still and cannot be whipped; it is used for pouring. Clotted cream is very thick and has the highest fat content. Sour cream has the same fat content as single cream, but it is cultured, giving it a thick texture and slightly sour, fresh taste. Crème fraîche is cultured fresh cream, which gives it a slightly sharp, acid taste. It has a fairly thick, spooning texture but it cannot be whipped. It can be heated.

Yogurt Varying in fat content, yogurt may be set or runny, with a thin or creamy texture. It tends to curdle when heated, although Greek (US strained plain) yogurt can be used for cooking.

Above:
Parmesan cheese is
very good for cooking and is also excellent grated
or shaved over pasta, risotto and other dishes.

Butter

There are two main types of butter – salted and unsalted (sweet). Unsalted is better for baking cakes and cookies.

Hard cheeses

These firm, tasty cheeses are good for cooking. They should have a dry rind. Store wrapped in baking parchment in the refrigerator for up to 2 weeks.

Cheddar There are many varieties of this classic sharp cheese – some strong, some mild. Its high fat content and good melting properties make it a great choice for cheese sauces.

Parmesan This cheese comes from the area around Parma in Italy and only cheeses with Parmigiano Reggiano stamped on the rind have this designation. It is a hard, dry cheese with a full, sweet flavour.

Gruyère This Swiss cheese with a dry texture and nutty flavour is good in cooking and for melting over dishes.

Manchego This Spanish ewe's milk cheese has a dry texture and a nutty, buttery taste.

Above: *There are many different types of cream, from thick to pourable.*

Semi-hard cheeses

These vary in softness depending on the type. Choose cheeses that feel springy and have firm rinds. Wrap in waxed paper and store in the refrigerator for 1–2 weeks.

Fontina This deep golden yellow Italian cheese has a pale brown rind and lots of little holes throughout the cheese. It melts fairly well but is not good for sauces.

Halloumi This salty Greek cheese has a firm, slightly rubbery texture and is perfect for grilling (broiling).

Blue cheese

These strong, often sharp, cheeses usually melt well and are good for cooking and flavouring sauces.

Stilton This strong, sharp cheese melts well into sauces and complements chicken and more robust meats.

Gorgonzola This Italian blue cheese has a rich, piquant flavour with a firm but creamy texture. It melts smoothly and can be used in a wide range of dishes.

Dolcelatte This Italian blue cheese has a milder flavour than Gorgonzola and a soft, creamy texture. It is good with summer fruit and can be used in cooking.

Soft and fresh cheeses

These mild, unripened cheeses should smell fresh. Store in a covered container in the refrigerator for up to 1 week.

Mozzarella This Italian cheese has a soft, elastic texture and mild, milky flavour and is good when melted. Baby balls of mozzarella (bocconcini) are also available.

Above: Stilton has a sharp, tangy flavour and creamy texture. It is good served on its own or used in salads and cooking.

Feta This white, firm Greek cheese has a crumbly texture and sharp, salty flavour. Feta does not melt easily and is not ideal for general cooking but is good used in salads.

Mascarpone This creamy, mild cheese has a high fat content and can be used in sweet and savoury recipes.

White rind cheeses

These creamy cheeses with a firm, white mould rind are delicious used fresh in salads or cooked.

Brie This French cheese is one of the best of the white rind cheeses. The flavour can be mild or extremely strong, tangy and creamy when ripe. Brie can be grilled (broiled), baked or coated in breadcrumbs and deep-fried.

Firm goat's cheese One of the most popular types is shaped in a log, often sold sliced into a white ring. It is excellent for slicing and melting. Soft goat's cheese, without the rind, has a milder flavour.

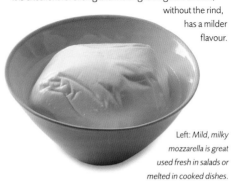

Eggs

Widely used in sweet and savoury cooking, eggs are incredibly versatile and are perfect for making simple meals such as omelettes or baked eggs.
Hens' eggs These can be boiled, poached, fried, scrambled or baked. They are widely used for baking. Buy the best you can afford – hens reared in better conditions produce better-tasting eggs.
Quails' eggs These small speckled eggs are similar in flavour to hens' eggs. They can be fried, poached or boiled and are useful for canapés.

Left: Mild, milky mozzarella is great used fresh in salads or melted in cooked dishes.

Fish and Shellfish

Full of flavour and quick to cook, fish and shellfish are delicious cooked simply. Always buy really fresh specimens: look for bright-eyed fish with plump flesh and bright, undamaged skin; they should not smell "fishy" but should have a faint aroma of the sea. Good fishmongers will scale, cut and fillet the fish for you. Choose lobsters and crabs that feel heavy for their size. Store fish and shellfish, covered, towards the bottom of the refrigerator, and use within a day of purchase.

Above: *Fresh anchovies are tasty marinated in lemon juice.*

Oily fish

The rich flesh of oily fish is extremely tasty and very good for you. Oily fish are rich in omega 3 fatty acids, which are an essential part of a healthy diet and are said to be good for the heart. Oily fish also contain less fat than most meat or poultry, and the fat is generally unsaturated.

Anchovies When available fresh, anchovies are delicious grilled (broiled) and served with a squeeze of lemon juice. Good quality salted anchovies are versatile and delicious in many dishes, particularly pasta sauces.

Mackerel These fish have iridescent skin and quite firm, brownish flesh. They can be baked whole, wrapped in baking parchment, with lemon and herbs, or marinated and grilled. The robust flavour of mackerel is enhanced by pungent spices, such as coriander and cumin.

Herring Smaller than mackerel, herring can be treated in much the same way. They are also delicious pickled.

Sardines These small fish are delicious fresh, cooked over a barbecue with lime or lemon juice and herbs.

Rich, meaty fish

This group of firm fish have a meaty texture. Some have a mild flavour, while others such as tuna are more robust.

Monkfish Tasty baked, pan-fried and grilled, this fish is usually sold prepared as monkfish tails, which have a firm, meaty texture and a delicate flavour. Ask the fishmonger to remove all traces of skin and membrane around the fish, as this turns very rubbery on cooking.

Sea bass This is an expensive fish but its flavour is well worth the cost. Try fillets pan-fried in a little butter and served with a squeeze of lime juice.

Tuna Fresh tuna is now more widely available – bluefin is the most prized, followed by yellowfin. It is best served rare. Steaks are best pan-fried for 1–2 minutes each side.

Swordfish Pink-tinged, meaty swordfish is excellent cooked over a barbecue, but be sure not to overcook it because the flesh becomes dry.

Red mullet You can recognise red mullet by the yellow stripe that runs along the body. It is an attractive fish with fine, delicious white flesh. The fillets are good pan-fried with the skin on and served with creamy mashed potato.

White fish

These fish have a firm yet delicate white flesh, excellent cooked simply with subtle or piquant flavouring.

Cod Stocks of cod in the sea are diminishing due to overfishing resulting in a rise in price. Large cod fillet has a firm texture and an almost milky quality to its flesh.

Plaice Cooked whole or as fillets, plaice can be fried, grilled, steamed or baked. It can be slightly bland, so add a piquant sauce or herbs and olive oil to perk it up.

Below: *Tuna steaks are great marinated in oil and lime juice and then grilled.*

Crab These crustaceans are cooked live, plunged into a pan of boiling water, which many people find off-putting. However, crab is also available ready-cooked. A crab yields a small amount of meat for its size, so allow 500g/1^{1}/$_{4}$lb weight of whole crab per person.

Lobster Like crabs, lobsters should be cooked live, so buy ready-cooked lobsters and split in half lengthways to extract the meat. Crack the claws with a hammer to extract the meat in the same way as for crab claws.

Haddock This flaky fish can be used instead of cod or in recipes calling for white fish. Smoked haddock is delicious but avoid the bright yellow dyed variety and go for the paler, undyed version.

Skate This fish has a hard, cartilaginous skeleton and no bones. It is sold as flat wings. Piquant capers are the perfect companion seasoning.

Prawns/shrimp There are many types of prawns of different sizes, cooked or raw, in the shell, or peeled. They are delicious pan-fried with chopped garlic and chilli. When large prawns are peeled, the black vein that runs along the back has to be removed and discarded. Brown shrimps must be used for potted shrimps.

Shellfish

There are several different types of shellfish. Molluscs have either one or two shells. Once dead, they deteriorate rapidly and can cause food poisoning. Because of this, they must always be perfectly fresh and cooked alive. Crustaceans, including crabs, lobsters and prawns (shrimp) have a protective shell that is shed occasionally as the creature grows. Store shellfish in the refrigerator and always use within 1–2 days.

Mussels Sweet, mild-tasting mussels need to be cleaned thoroughly before cooking. Wash or scrub in cold water and pull off any black hairs (the beard) protruding from the shell. Tap any open mussels on a work surface and discard any that do not close straight away, along with any broken shells. When cooked, discard any unopened mussels.

Scallops Tender, delicately flavoured scallops need very little cooking. Simply pan-fry for 1–2 minutes on each side over high heat. Choose scallops with a sweet smell; this indicates freshness. To open, hold the scallop shell, curved side down, and insert the tip of an oyster knife between the two shells. Twist to prise the shells apart, then cut through the muscle holding the scallop in the shell, and remove any muscle and membrane from the meat and coral.

Extracting meat from a cooked crab

1 Lay the crab on its back and twist off the legs and claws. Use a hammer to break open the claws and legs, and pick out the meat.

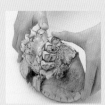

2 There is a flap or opening on the body – carefully lift this up and twist it off, gently pulling the crab out of its shell.

3 Discard the gills from the side of the body and spoon the brown meat from the main body section and from the shell.

Meat and Poultry

If possible, buy organic meat and poultry. It is better to eat less meat of better quality than a larger quantity of cheaper meat. Animals and birds that have been raised in a good environment and fed on quality feed produce better-tasting meat than mass-reared, unhappy livestock. When you are cooking with only a few ingredients, each one needs to have an excellent flavour and texture.

Pork

Comparatively inexpensive, pork is a very versatile meat. It is generally tender and has an excellent flavour.

Shoulder, leg and loin The shoulder or leg is the best cut for roasting. To make good crackling, ensure that the rind is thoroughly dry and rub it generously with sea salt. Loin or shoulder chops are suited to pan-frying or braising.

Belly Traditionally quite fatty, belly pork is good roasted and braised. It is especially tasty with Asian flavourings.

Spare ribs Meaty pork ribs can be delicious marinated and then roasted or barbecued with a sticky glaze.

Pork tenderloin A lean, long piece of meat, the tenderloin can dry out during cooking. Wrap it in bacon to keep it moist before roasting.

Bacon Available smoked or unsmoked. If possible, buy dry-cured bacon. Streaky (fatty) bacon has a higher percentage of fat than back bacon, and can be cooked to a crisp-fried texture. Back bacon has larger rashers (strips) and a balance of lean to fatty areas.

Left: Rolled belly of pork is a fatty joint that is succulent either slowly roasted or pot-roasted. Serve with piquant flavours, which go well with the fatty meat.

Above: *Entrecôte steaks are cut from beef sirloin, have a rich colour and are delicious pan-fried or grilled.*

Gammon This smoky meat is available in a whole piece or as steaks. Whole gammon may need soaking before cooking. Steaks can be pan-fried or grilled (broiled).

Pancetta This traditional Italian cured bacon comes in rashers (strips) or cut into dice. It can be pan-fried.

Prosciutto This dry-cured ham is eaten raw, cut into very thin slices. It can be cooked, usually as a topping on dishes or to enclose other ingredients before grilling or roasting.

Beef

This well-flavoured, versatile meat is good for stewing, roasting, grilling (broiling), pan-frying and stir-frying.

Fillet/beef tenderloin, forerib, topside and silverside/pot roast These are best roasted. To make the most of the flavour, serve medium, not well-done.

Steaks Sirloin, T-bone, porterhouse, fillet (beef tenderloin) and sirloin are best pan-fried over a high heat.

Shin or leg/shank, chuck and brisket These cuts can be quite tough and are best stewed slowly to tenderize them and bring out their excellent flavour.

Mince/ground meat This is a very versatile ingredient for meat sauces, chilli con carne, meatballs, pasta dishes, samosas, pies and many other dishes.

Lamb

Delicious in roasts and superb grilled (broiled), pan-fried and stewed, lamb is one of the best-loved of all meats.

Best end of neck, leg, shoulder and saddle These are the best cuts for roasting. Best end of neck can be cut into chops. Shoulder contains more fat than leg but it has an excellent flavour. Spring lamb has the best taste.

Chump chops and leg steaks These have a full flavour and can be either grilled (broiled) or pan-fried.

Sausages and offal/variety meats

Offal refers to all offcuts from the carcass but in everyday use, this usually means liver and kidneys.

Sausages There are many types of fresh sausage from around the world. Depending on the variety, they may be fried, grilled (broiled) or baked.

Liver Pigs', lambs' or calves' liver has a strong flavour and are good pan-fried, with bacon and mashed potato.

Kidneys Lambs' kidneys are lighter in flavour than pigs'. They should be halved and the central core discarded before they are pan-fried or used in stews and pies.

Poultry and game birds

Many people prefer the lighter flavour of poultry and game birds to that of red meat.

Chicken Buy organic or free-range chicken. Choose smooth-skinned, unblemished plump birds.

Carving a roast chicken

1 Leave the bird to rest for 10 minutes, then remove the legs and cut through the joints to make the thigh and drumstick portions.

2 Remove the wings, then carve the meat off the breasts, working down on either side of the breastbone. Use a gentle sawing action.

Poussin These baby chickens are perfect roasted or spatchcocked , then cooked over the barbecue.

Duck Traditionally, duck can be very fatty with a fairly small amount of meat. An average duck will serve two or three people. Duck breasts and legs are a good choice for simple cooking.

Pheasant One pheasant will serve two. The breast meat is fairly dry and needs constant basting during roasting. Choose pheasants that are no older than six months; older birds are tough.

Below from left: Corn-fed, free-range and organic chickens have a good flavour.

Herbs

Invaluable in a huge number of sweet and savoury recipes, herbs add flavour, colour and contrast to many dishes. Fresh herbs are widely available and their flavour is superior to that of dried herbs. Many are easy to grow yourself at home – either in the garden or in a pot on the windowsill. You can grow them from seed, or buy them already growing in pots from supermarkets and garden stores.

Robust herbs

These strong-tasting, often pungent herbs are good with meat and well-flavoured dishes. Use in moderation.

Bay leaves These shiny, aromatic leaves can be added to meat dishes, roasts, casseroles and stews before cooking. Roughly tear the leaves before you add them, then remove before serving. They are an essential part of a bouquet garni.

Rosemary This pungent herb is delicious with lamb – insert a few sprigs into slits in the skin of a leg of lamb and the flavour will really penetrate the meat during roasting. For other recipes, use whole leaves or chop them finely.

Above: Rosemary and sage have a robust, pungent flavour that goes well with strongly flavoured, fatty meats such as lamb and pork.

Freezing herbs

This is a great way of preserving fresh herbs because it retains their natural flavour. Use in cooked dishes only. Chop the herbs and place about one tablespoonful in each compartment of an ice cube tray. Pour over water to cover and freeze. To use, simply add a herb ice cube to the pan and stir.

Making a bouquet garni

This classic flavouring for stews, casseroles and soups is very easy to make. Using a piece of string, tie together a fresh bay leaf and a sprig each of parsley and thyme. Alternatively, tie the herbs in a square of muslin (cheesecloth).

Thyme One of the traditional herbs used in a bouquet garni, thyme has small leaves and some types have woody stems. It has a strong, pungent flavour. Add whole sprigs to meat dishes or strip the leaves and use in pasta sauces.

Sage Peppery tasting sage has large, slightly furry leaves. It is a great companion for pork and is excellent with potatoes and also in tomato and garlic pasta dishes. Ravioli served with a little melted butter and warmed sage leaves is particularly delicious. Use in moderation because its flavour can be overpowering if used in excess.

Chives Long slender chives have a distinct onion-like flavour. Chives are best snipped with scissors. They are good in potato salads and egg and dairy dishes.

Oregano One of the few herbs that responds well to drying, oregano is great for tomato-based sauces and with other vegetables. It is also good with chicken.

Lavender This can be used sparingly to complement chicken dishes and also in sweet recipes such as drinks and desserts. The stalks and leaves can be used as well as the flowers, which make a pretty garnish.

Leafy herbs

These delicate, soft-leafed herbs have a fragrant flavour. Use in salads or add towards the end of cooking time.

Basil Widely used in Italian cookery, basil has delicate leaves and should be added at the end of cooking. It has a slightly aniseed flavour that goes well with chicken, fish, all types of vegetables and pasta. It is one of the main ingredients of pesto.

Coriander/cilantro The deep, almost woody, flavour of coriander is superb in spicy dishes. It is good in Thai-style soups and curries, meat and egg dishes, as well as more robustly flavoured fish dishes.

Parsley Flat or curly leafed, parsley is one of the most versatile herbs and adds flavour to most savoury dishes. The flat-leafed variety has a stronger flavour and it can be used as an ingredient in its own right to make soup.

Mint There are many different varieties of mint, including apple mint and spearmint.It grows easily and goes well with lamb, desserts and drinks.

Tarragon This fragrant herb has a strong aniseed flavour and is most often paired with chicken and fish.

Chervil This pretty herb has a mild aniseed flavour that goes well with fish, chicken, cheese and creamy savoury dishes. It is also good in salads.

Below: *Mint has a cool and refreshing flavour and is used in both sweet and savoury dishes.*

Below: *Dill has a sweet, aromatic fragrance and is particularly good used in fish and egg dishes.*

Left: *Delicate, fragrant basil is the perfect flavouring to use with tomatoes.*

Fragrant herbs

These distinctive herbs have a strong, aromatic scent and flavour and suit many different kinds of dishes.

Kaffir lime leaves These dark green leaves are used to impart a citrus flavour to many South-east Asian soups and curries. Add the leaves whole, torn or finely shredded.

Lemon balm With a distinctive lemon flavour and fragrance, this herb complements all ingredients that go well with citrus fruit or juice. Lemon balm makes a good addition to fish, chicken and vegetable dishes as well as sweet drinks and desserts. Use in moderation.

Dill This pretty, feathery herb has a distinctive flavour that is perfect with fish, chicken and egg dishes. It also goes very well with potatoes, courgettes (zucchini) and cucumber. It should be added to dishes just before serving because its mild flavour diminishes with cooking.

Spices and Aromatics

These flavourings play a very important role when cooking with a limited number of ingredients, adding a warmth and roundness of flavour to simple dishes. It is difficult to have every spice to hand, but a few key spices will be enough to create culinary magic. Black pepper is an essential seasoning in every storecupboard; cumin seeds, coriander seeds, dried chillies and turmeric are also good basics.

Above: Saffron has a delicate fragrance and imparts a pale golden colour to both sweet and savoury dishes.

Dried spices

Store spices in airtight jars or containers in a cool, dark place. Buy small quantities that will be used up fairly quickly because flavours diminish with age. Check the sell-by dates of the spices in your store cupboard (pantry) and throw away any spices that are old or no longer fragrant; there is little point in using old, tasteless spices to flavour food because the results will not be satisfactory.

Pepper Black pepper is one of the most commonly used spices. It should always be freshly ground because, once ground, it loses its flavour quickly. It is used in almost all savoury recipes but can also be used to flavour shortbread and to bring out the flavour of fruit such as pineapple and strawberries. Green peppercorns have a mild flavour. They are available dried or preserved in brine and are excellent for flavouring pâtés and meat dishes. White pepper is hotter than green, but less aromatic than black.

Chilli flakes Crushed dried red chillies can be added to, or sprinkled over, all kinds of dishes – from stir-fries and grilled (broiled) meats to pasta sauces and pizza.

Cayenne pepper This fiery, piquant spice is made from a dried hot red chilli, so use sparingly. It is excellent in cheese dishes and creamy soups and sauces.

Paprika An essential seasoning for Hungarian goulash and used in many Spanish dishes, paprika is available in a mild and hot form. It has a slightly sweet flavour.

Saffron This expensive spice is the dried stigma of a crocus flower, and is available in strands or ground. Saffron strands have a superior flavour and are best infused in a little hot liquid, such as milk or water, before being added to a recipe. Saffron has a distinct but delicate flavour. It is used sparingly in all kinds of dishes, including paella, curry, risotto, rice pudding and baking. Be wary of very cheap saffron because it is probably not the true spice and will not offer the rich, rounded flavour of the real thing.

Below: Sweet paprika is the mildest of all the chilli powders and can be used to add a rich flavour and colour to savoury dishes.

Mustard seeds These may be black, brown or white. They are used to make the condiment mustard and are also used as a flavouring in cooking. Black mustard seeds are added to Indian dishes, for their crunchy texture as well as flavour. Try adding a few mustard seeds to bread dough to give it a spicy kick.

Cumin This warm, pungent spice is widely used in Indian and North African cooking. Cumin works well with meats and a variety of vegetables, particularly robust-tasting sweet potatoes, squashes and cabbage.

Caraway seeds These small dark seeds have a fennel-like flavour. They are very versatile and make a lively addition to savoury breads and sweet cakes, while also complementing strongly flavoured sausage dishes and vegetables such as cabbage.

Fennel seeds These pretty little green seeds have a sweet, aniseed-like flavour that pairs well with chicken and robust fish dishes. It also tastes good in breads.

Coriander Available whole or ground, this warm, aromatic spice is delicious with most meats, particularly lamb. It is widely used in Indian and Asian cooking and is frequently paired with cumin. When combined, ground coriander and cumin make an excellent spice rub.

Below: *Turmeric root is hard and must be ground to make the familiar bright yellow spice used in Indian cooking.*

Above: *Mustard seeds and cumin seeds have a warm, spicy aroma. Buy them whole, then grind them as you need them.*

Turmeric Made from dried turmeric root, the ground spice is bright yellow with a peppery, slightly earthy flavour. It is used in many Indian recipes.

Garam masala This Indian mixture of ground roasted spices is usually made from cumin, coriander, cardamom and black pepper. Ready mixed garam masala is widely available, although the flavour is better when the spices are freshly roasted and ground.

Chinese five spice This is a mixture of ground spices, including anise pepper, cassia, fennel seeds, star anise and cloves. It is used in Chinese cookery, particularly to season pork and chicken dishes. Chinese five spice is a powerful mixture and should be used sparingly.

Salt

Probably the most important of all seasonings, salt is an essential ingredient in almost every cuisine. It has been used for many years, not only to flavour and bring out the taste of other foods, but to preserve them as well. Cured fish and meat, such as salt cod, prosciutto, salt beef and bacon, are preserved in salt to draw out moisture and prevent them from decomposing.

The type of salt used is important – rock salt or sea salt does not have added chemicals, which are often found in table salt. Rock salt is available in crystal form and can be ground in a mill, or refined to cooking salt. Sea salt has a strong, salty taste and it is used in smaller amounts.

Above: *Cinnamon sticks can be added whole to hot drinks, stews and casseroles to add a warm, spicy flavour.*

Green cardamom This fragrant spice is widely used in Indian and North African cooking to flavour both sweet and savoury dishes. The papery green pods enclose little black seeds that are easily scraped out and can be crushed in a mortar with a pestle if required.

Cinnamon This warm spice is available in sticks and ground into powder and has many uses in savoury and sweet recipes. Add sticks to stews, casseroles and other liquid dishes, then remove them before serving. Use ground cinnamon in baking, desserts and drinks.

Ginger The ground, dried spice is particularly useful for baking. For a fresher flavour in savoury recipes and drinks, it is best to use fresh root ginger.

Nutmeg This large aromatic seed has a spicy flavour, which adds a warm spiciness to milk, egg and cream dishes and enhances the flavour of spinach. Nutmeg is available ready ground, but the flavour is far better when the spice is freshly grated. Try sprinkling a little grated nutmeg over milk-based soups before serving.

Mace This spice is the casing of the nutmeg – it has a similar flavour but is slightly milder. Mace is great for flavouring butter for savoury dishes and is an essential ingredient in potted shrimps.

Star anise This pretty, star-shaped spice has a strong aniseed flavour. It is widely used in Chinese and Asian cooking and is a great partner for pork and chicken. It is also good for flavouring rice – simply add a single star anise to the cooking water. It can be used to flavour sweet dishes such as ice creams and jellies.

Allspice This berry has a warm, slightly cinnamon-clove flavour. It is more readily available in its ground form and can be used in both savoury and sweet cooking. It goes particularly well in winter recipes and fruit cake.

Cloves Available whole or ground these dried flower buds are used in savoury and sweet dishes. Ham is particularly tasty studded with whole cloves before baking, while the ground spice is suitable for cakes and cookies. Ground cloves are strong, so use sparingly.

Juniper berries These small, dark-purple berries are the main flavouring in gin. Add a few juniper berries to meaty stews and casseroles to give a fragrant, spicy kick.

Vanilla Dried vanilla pods (beans) are long and black, encasing hundreds of tiny black seeds. Warm the whole pod in milk, or place in a jar of sugar, to allow the flavour to infuse (steep), or split the pods, scrape out the seeds and add to cakes, desserts and ice cream. Natural vanilla extract is distilled from vanilla pods and is a useful alternative to pods. Vanilla extract tends to have a better flavour than vanilla essence, which can be quite overpowering. Some flavourings are not actually vanilla, but a synthetic alternative.

Above: *For the best flavour, grate whole nutmegs as and when you need the spice, using a special small grater.*

Fresh spices and aromatics

These wonderful flavourings are widely used in many dishes and add a rich, round, aromatic taste.

Fresh root ginger This pale-brown root should be peeled and then sliced, shredded, finely chopped or grated as required. It is used in curries, stir-fries, and grilled (broiled) and braised dishes. Choose plump roots and store in the refrigerator for up to 6 weeks. Preserved and crystallized ginger can be used in sweet dishes.

Galangal Similar in appearance to fresh root ginger, but often slimmer and with a pink-purple tinge, galangal is used in Thai and Indonesian cooking. Treat as for fresh root ginger, but store for a maximum of 3 weeks.

Above: *Fresh root ginger has a pungent, zesty flavour that is delicious used in savoury dishes – either raw or cooked.*

Above: *Fresh lemon grass is widely used in Thai cooking.*

Lemon grass This woody pale green stalk is excellent with fish and chicken, and can be used to flavour sweet dishes such as ice cream. Either bruise the bulbous end of the stalk and add whole to curries and soups, or finely slice or chop the end of the stalk and stir into the dish.

Garlic A member of the onion family and therefore often included as a vegetable, garlic also deserves mention as an aromatic for its role in flavouring all kinds of savoury dishes, raw or cooked. The potency of garlic depends on how it has been prepared. Crushed garlic gives the most powerful flavour, while finely chopping, shredding or slicing gives a slightly less strong result. Use garlic to flavour salad dressings or dips, or use whole, peeled cloves to flavour oils or vinegars. (Garlic is renowned for lingering on the breath after consumption; chewing fresh parsley is said to help counteract this.)

Ready-made spice mixes

There is an excellent selection of ready-made spice mixes available that make great short-cut flavouring ingredients for savoury dishes.

Harissa This North Arfrican spice paste is made of chillies, garlic, coriander, caraway, olive oil and other spices. It is delicious with oily fish as well as meat.

Chermoula This is another North African spice paste, which includes coriander, parsley, chilli and saffron.

Cajun seasoning This spice mixture made of black and white pepper, garlic, cumin and paprika is good for rubbing into meat before cooking over a barbecue.

Jerk seasoning This Caribbean spice blend is made of dry spices and goes well with chicken and pork.

Above: *Harissa paste can be used to flavour savoury dishes, such as soups and stews, or as a marinade for meat and fish.*

Other Flavourings

As well as herbs, spices and aromatics, there are a number of basic flavourings that are widely used in both sweet and savoury cooking. Sweeteners, such as sugar and honey, and flavourings, such as chocolate and alcohol, are mainly used in sweet dishes, but they can also be used in savoury dishes. Sauces and condiments, such as soy sauce, can be used to enhance the taste of savoury ingredients.

Sugars and sweet spreads

Refined and raw sugars and sweet spreads such as honey and marmalade can all be used to sweeten and flavour.

Granulated This refined white sugar has large crystals. It is used for sweetening drinks and everyday cooking; it can also be used as a crunchy cookie or cake topping, or stirred into crumble mixtures for extra texture.

Caster/Superfine sugar This fine-grained white sugar is most frequently used in baking. Its fine texture is particularly well suited to making cakes and cookies.

Icing/Confectioners' sugar The finest of all the refined sugars, this sugar has a light, powdery texture. It is used for making icing and sweetening flavoured creams. It is also good for dusting on cakes, desserts and cookies as a decoration.

Below: *Sugar cubes and rock sugar are most frequently used to sweeten drinks.*

Demerara sugar This golden sugar consists of large crystals with a rich, slightly honeyish flavour. It is great for adding a crunchy texture to cookies.

Brown sugars These dark, unrefined sugars have a rich, caramel flavour. There are different types including light and dark muscovado (brown) sugar and dark brown molasses sugar. The darker the sugar, the more intense its flavour. Always check you are buying unrefined sugar because "brown" sugars are often actually white sugar that has been coloured after refining.

Left: *Granulated sugar has larger crystals than caster sugar but both are good for making cakes and desserts.*

Below: *Golden demerara sugar and soft brown sugar have a moist texture and rich, more rounded flavour.*

Honey Clear honey is used to flavour desserts, cakes and cookies as well as savoury dressings. It also makes a good base for barbecue sauces and glazes for chicken or meat.

Marmalade Most often served as a sweet spread, marmalade can also make an interesting ingredient. Try orange marmalade as the base for a quick sauce to serve with duck.

Above: *Sweet, golden honey is perfect for flavouring sweet and savoury dishes.*

Chocolate

There are many different types of chocolate, each with its own unique flavour. They can all be used in many ways – grated, chopped or melted, and stirred into ice creams, or used for desserts, sauces or in baking. Always choose plain (semisweet) chocolate with at least 70 per cent cocoa solids for a good flavour. Children often prefer the milder flavour of milk chocolate. White chocolate has a low cocoa solids content and is sweet with a very mild flavour. Chocolate spread is also a useful ingredient. It can be melted and stirred into ice cream, custard or drinks, or used in many desserts.

Below: *White, dark and milk chocolate are all popularly used in desserts, cookies, cakes, drinks and sweet sauces.*

Edible flowers

Many flowers are edible and can be used as ingredients. Roses and violets look delightful frosted and are used to decorate cakes and desserts. Simply brush the clean flower heads or petals with a little egg white and sprinkle with caster (superfine) sugar and leave to dry. Plain rose petals can be used to flavour sugar syrups; rosewater and orange flower water are readily available and convenient and easy to use. Fragrant lavender heads can be left to infuse in cream for about 30 minutes, imparting their flavour.

Flowers can also be used in savoury dishes. Nasturtiums, pansies, marigolds and herb flowers, such as chives, are used to flavour salads.

Coffee

To achieve a strong coffee flavour, use good quality espresso. You do not need an espresso machine for this because espresso coffee is sold for use in cafetières or filter machines. Make a double-strength brew to flavour desserts, sauces, cakes and cookies.

Almond essence/extract

This distinctive-tasting flavouring is perfect for cakes, cookies and desserts, and is also used for flavouring cream that will be served with fruit desserts. It is very strong, so use sparingly.

Above: *Buy good quality espresso coffee beans and grind them freshly to make a really strong brew for flavouring desserts and cakes. Alternatively, use ready-ground espresso coffee.*

Alcohol

Wine, spirits, beer and cider add body to both sweet and savoury dishes. Wines and spirits can be used to perk up cooked dishes and to macerate fruits and enliven desserts. Beer and cider are more widely used in savoury dishes such as stews and casseroles.

Wine Fruity red wines can be used to enrich meat dishes, tomato sauces and gravies. Dry white wine goes well with chicken or fish dishes. Sweet white wines and sparkling wines can be used to make jellies and sweet sauces.

Port Ruby port can be added to sauces for red meats – it is richer and sweeter than red wine, so use more sparingly. Port is also suitable for macerating summer fruits.

Sherry Dry, medium or sweet sherry can be used in savoury and sweet recipes. Add a dash to gravies and meat sauces or add a couple of spoonfuls to a rich fruit cake or dessert.

Marsala This Italian fortified wine is used to flavour desserts such as tiramisu and is also good in meat dishes.

Spirits Use rum and brandy for flavouring meat sauces, ice creams and cakes. Clear spirits, such as vodka and gin, can be used for sorbets; add a splash of vodka to tomato-based pasta dishes and fish dishes to give an extra kick. Irish cream liqueurs have a velvet-like texture that is excellent in creams, ice creams and cake fillings. Sweet fruit liqueurs are great used in desserts.

Right: Almond-flavoured amaretto is delicious in creams and ice creams.

Above: Sherry and Marsala are classic flavourings for desserts such as trifle and Italian tiramisu. They are also used in meat dishes and can add a rich, round flavour to meat sauces.

Preserved fruit and nuts

Above: Preserved lemons have an intense flavour.

Preserved lemons A classic in North African cooking, the lemons are preserved whole or in large pieces in a mixture of salt and spices. The chopped peel is usually added to chicken dishes to add an intense, sharp, citrus flavour.

Dried fruit Dried apricots, prunes, figs, currants, sultanas (golden raisins) and raisins can be added to savoury dishes and meat stews to impart a rich, sweet flavour. They are also good for adding flavour and body to sweet desserts, cakes and cookies.

Nuts Almonds, walnuts and pine nuts are useful for savoury dishes such as salads, vegetable dishes, pastes and dips, as well as in desserts and baking.

Coconut milk Thin, creamy coconut milk is made from pulped coconut and is widely used in Thai and Asian cooking, particularly in curries and soups.

Sauces and condiments

Not only are sauces and condiments perfect for serving with main dishes at the table, they are also great for adding extra flavour and bite to simple dishes during cooking.

Mustard Wholegrain mustard containing whole mustard seeds has a sweet, fruity taste and makes a mild, flavourful salad dressing. French Dijon mustard has a fairly sharp, piquant flavour which complements red meat and makes a sharply flavoured dressing. English mustard may be purchased as a dry powder or ready prepared and is excellent added to cheese dishes, or used to enliven bland creamy sauces.

Tomato purée/paste This concentrated purée is an essential in every storecupboard (pantry). It is great for adding flavour, and sometimes body, to sauces and stews.

Passata/bottled strained tomatoes This Italian product, made of sieved tomatoes, has a fairly thin consistency and makes a good base for a tomato sauce.

Tomato ketchup Add a splash of this strong table condiment to tomato sauces for a sweet-sour flavour.

Worcestershire sauce This thin, brown, very spicy sauce brings a piquant flavour to casseroles, stews and soups. It can also be used to perk up cheese dishes.

Below: Wholegrain mustard can be used in dressings and cheese sauces – adding real bite and interest to their flavour.

Right: Dark and light soy sauce are the perfect flavourings for Chinese and Asian dishes.

Below: Sun-dried tomato paste can add extra flavour to tomato sauces, and meat and vegetable soups and stews.

Curry paste There are many ready-made curry pastes, including those for classic Indian and Thai curries. They can also be used to spice up dishes such as burgers.

Sweet chilli sauce You can add this sweet, spicy dipping sauce to stir-fries and braised chicken dishes, and it can be used as a glaze for chicken or prawns before grilling (broiling) or cooking over a barbecue.

Soy sauce Made from fermented soy beans, soy sauce is salty and a little adds a rich, rounded flavour to Asian-style stir-fries, glazes and sauces.

Teriyaki marinade This Japanese marinade has a sweet, salty flavour. Use it to marinate meat, chicken and fish before frying; the leftover marinade will cook down to make a delicious, sticky sauce.

Oyster sauce Add this thick Chinese sauce with a sweet, meaty taste to stir-fries and braised dishes.

Pesto Use fresh pesto, made with basil, garlic, pine nuts and Parmesan cheese, on pasta or to flavour sauces, soups, stews and dressings. There are also variations such as red pesto made with roasted red (bell) peppers.

Kitchen Basics

Keep a well-stocked storecupboard (pantry) and you will be able to cook almost anything at any time. However, this does not mean overloading your storage space with a vast range of ingredients. A selection of well-chosen, essential ingredients is more important than a cupboard full of obscure, out-of-date items that have been used once and then forgotten. The following are some useful basic ingredients that will be invaluable in every kitchen; try to remember to check cupboards regularly and be vigilant about throwing away out-of-date ingredients and replenishing them with fresh ones.

Flour

This is an essential ingredient in every kitchen. There are many different types, which serve many purposes in both sweet and savoury cooking – from baking cakes to thickening gravy and making cheese sauce.

Wheat flours Plain (all-purpose) flour can be used in most recipes, including sauces. Self-raising (self-rising) flour has a raising agent added and is useful for cakes and other baking recipes. Wholemeal flour is available as plain (all-purpose) or self-raising (self-rising). Strong bread flour contains more gluten than plain flour, making it more suitable for making breads.

Right: (Clockwise from top) There are many different types of flour for different purposes, including strong bread flour, French bread flour, self-raising flour and plain flour. For general kitchen use, plain flour is probably the most versatile.

Gluten-free flours For those with an allergy to gluten, which is found in wheat and other grains, gluten-free flour is an invaluable ingredient. It is widely available from most large supermarkets and health food stores.

Cornflour/cornstarch This very fine white flour is useful for thickening sauces and stabilizing egg mixtures, such as custard, to prevent them curdling. A little cornflour is first blended with cold water or another liquid to make a smooth, runny paste, which is then stirred into a hot sauce, soup or stew and boiled until it thickens.

Raising agents Self-raising flour contains raising agents, normally baking powder, which give a light texture to cakes and cookies. You can add baking powder to plain flour to achieve the same result. The baking powder reacts with liquids and heat during cooking and produces carbon-dioxide bubbles, which make the mixture rise.

Oils

Essential both for cooking and adding flavour, there are many different types of oil, all of which have their own character and use in the kitchen. Every cook should have a bottle of oil for cooking, and also oils for drizzling and flavouring.

Olive oil Extra virgin olive oil, made from the first pressing of the olives, has the best, most pronounced flavour and is the most expensive type. It is best reserved for condiments or salad dressings. Ordinary olive oil is generally the third or fourth pressing of the oil and is better used in cooking. Light olive oil is paler and milder in flavour than ordinary olive oil and is ideal for making lightly flavoured salad dressings.

Groundnut oil This virtually flavourless oil is used for frying, baking and making dressings such as mayonnaise.

Corn oil Golden-coloured corn oil has a fairly strong flavour and can be used in most types of cooking.

Below: Flavoured oils are invaluable in the minimalist kitchen – providing extra taste without having to add extra ingredients.

Left: Rich, dark sesame oil and spicy chilli oil can be added to stir-fries and dressings to add flavour.

Vegetable oil This is a blend of oils, usually including corn oil and other vegetable oils. It is quite flavourless and useful in most types of cooking.

Sesame oil Sesame and toasted sesame seed oils both have strong flavours and should be used sparingly when cooking.

Hazelnut and walnut oils Both are quite strongly flavoured and useful as dressings rather than for cooking. They are delicious drizzled over cooked fish, poultry or vegetables, or used in salad dressings.

Flavoured oils There are many types and brands of flavoured oils. Look out for those using a good-quality olive oil as the base.

Chilli oil This is available in various styles – it adds a pleasing spicy kick to all sorts of dishes such as pasta, fish and salads. Add a drizzle just before serving the food.

Garlic oil This is a good alternative to fresh garlic. It has a fairly strong flavour so it should be used with care.

Lemon-infused oil This is excellent with fish, chicken and pasta, and for salad dressings.

Right: Extra virgin olive oil has a rich, fruity taste and is perfect for drizzling over dishes and making dressings.

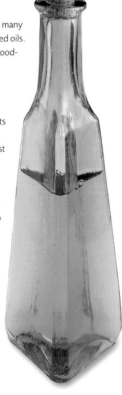

Pasta and noodles

These are invaluable storecupboard (pantry) ingredients that can be used as the base of many hot and cold dishes.

Pasta Dried pasta keeps for months in an airtight container – check the packet for information on keeping quality. There is a wide variety of pasta in all shapes and

sizes. Egg pasta is enriched with egg yolks and it has a richer flavour than plain pasta. Generally, the choice depends on personal taste – use whichever type you have in the cupboard. Cook pasta at a rolling boil in plenty of salted water. Fresh pasta cooks very quickly and is available chilled. It can be stored in the refrigerator for several days, or in the freezer for several months.

Above: *Dried pasta is a handy kitchen standby and can be used to make hot, hearty dishes or light, tasty salads.*

Egg noodles Made from wheat flour and eggs, these may be thick, medium or thin. Use them for stir-fries or as an accompaniment to Chinese and Asian dishes.

Below: *Egg noodles have a nutty taste and can be served hot in Asian-style stir-fries and soups, and cold in salads.*

Above:
Polenta is widely used in Italian-style dishes and makes a good alternative to pasta. It can be served as an accompaniment or made into a main dish.

Rice noodles These translucent white noodles are a good alternative to wheat noodles – particularly for those on a gluten-free diet. They are available as broad flat or thin noodles that can be added to stir-fries and soups as well as used cold as the base for salads. Rice noodles are easy to prepare because they don't need to be cooked. Simply soak in boiling water for about 5 minutes, then stir-fry, add to soups or toss with salad ingredients.

Couscous and polenta

Like pasta and noodles, couscous and polenta can be served as an accompaniment or can act as the base of many dishes. They have a mild flavour, and go particularly well with other, strongly flavoured ingredients.

Couscous Made from durum wheat, couscous is often regarded as a type of pasta. Traditional couscous needed long steaming before serving, but the majority of brands available in supermarkets today are "instant" and need only brief soaking in water. It is the classic accompaniment to Moroccan tagines, but also goes well with all kinds of meat, fish and vegetable stews. It makes an excellent base for salads.

Polenta This is made from finely ground cornmeal. It is cooked with water and served either soft (rather like mashed potato) or left to set and then cut into pieces that can be grilled (broiled) or fried. Quick-cook and ready-made polenta are available in most supermarkets and can be made into simple, hearty dishes. It is best served with flavourful ingredients.

Rice

This versatile grain can be served as an accompaniment, or form the base of both sweet and savoury dishes.

Long-grain rice The narrow grains of white rice cook to a light, fluffy texture and are generally served as an accompaniment to main dishes. They also make a perfect base for other dishes such as stir-fries and salads.

Short-grain rice There are several types of short, stubby, polished rice such as pudding rice and sushi rice. These usually have a high starch content and cook into tender grains that cling together and can be shaped easily.

Thai Jasmine rice This white, slightly sticky rice has a scented flavour. Serve with Thai curries or in stir-fries.

Risotto rice This rice has medium-length polished grains. The grains can absorb a great deal of liquid while still retaining their shape. There are several types of risotto rice, including the popular arborio and carnaroli. When cooking risotto rice, it is imperative to stir it regularly. Liquid or stock should be added periodically throughout cooking to prevent the rice sticking to the pan and burning.

Basmati rice This long-grain rice is widely used in Indian cooking. It is aromatic and cooks to give separated, fluffy grains. Brown basmati rice is also available.

Below: *Canned beans are nutritious and versatile and can be used in hearty stews, healthy salads or tasty dips and pâtés.*

Vegetables, beans and lentils

Dried, canned and bottled vegetables, beans and lentils are very versatile and are a useful storecupboard standby.

Above: *Canned tomatoes are a real storecupboard standby.*

Canned tomatoes Available chopped or whole, canned tomatoes are an essential item in every kitchen. They are very versatile and can be used to make sauces, pasta dishes, pizza toppings, soups and stews. Look out for canned Italian pomodorino tomatoes in a thick juice; they make a superbly rich sauce.

Dried mushrooms Dried wild mushrooms such as porcini and morels are a useful alternative to fresh, seasonal mushrooms, which are not always available. They add a rich flavour to pasta dishes and casseroles.

Bottled antipasti Red (bell) peppers, aubergines (eggplant), mushrooms and artichoke hearts preserved in olive oil with garlic and herbs are a classic Italian appetizer but can make a tasty addition to salads and pasta dishes.

Above: *Juicy black olives add bite to sauces and salads.*

Olives Black and green, olives bring a rich flavour to salads and pasta dishes; they also make a quick and easy appetizer when served with salami and bread.

Red lentils Compared to most other dried beans, red lentils have a relatively short cooking time and are ideal for making a quick and tasty Indian-style dhal.

Canned pulses Dried pulses such as flageolet beans, chickpeas, red kidney beans, cannellini beans and butter (lima) beans have a long shelf-life but require lengthy preparation: soaking overnight and then long boiling. The canned alternatives simply need to be rinsed in cold water, and can then be used in hot dishes or used to make salads.

Short-cut Ingredients

There are some useful products available in supermarkets and food stores that can help you save valuable time in the kitchen. These ingredients are usually pre-prepared in some way, taking the time and effort out of preparation. They provide a quick base for dishes so you will need fewer ingredients and can spend less time on shopping and cooking, and more time relaxing and eating.

Pastry Ready-made pastry is widely available in supermarkets and can make quick work of tarts, pies and filled pastries. Shortcrust, sweet shortcrust, puff and filo pastry can all be purchased frozen or chilled and ready to use. They are usually of excellent quality, giving delicious results. Some pastries are even ready-rolled so all you have to do is open the packet, cut, fold and fill the pastry, and then bake it in the oven until crisp and golden.

Cookie dough Cartons of chocolate chip cookie dough can be useful for many sweet recipes. It can be shaped and baked to make plain cookies or, more imaginatively, they could be coated with a topping or sandwiched together with a chocolate filling or ice cream to make a decadent treat or a sumptuous dessert. The dough can also be rolled thinly and used to line muffin tins (pans) to make a crisp cookie cup to fill with ice cream for dessert. Bitesize pieces of the cookie dough can be stirred into a vanilla ice cream mix to make cookie dough ice cream.

Marzipan Good quality marzipan is available in most supermarkets. It is perfect for decorating cakes, but it can be used in many other ways as well. Try rolling it out thinly and using it as a tart base under fruit, or chop it into small pieces and add to cookies and cakes.

Right (from top to bottom): Ready-made filo, shortcrust, puff and flaky pastries are available fresh and frozen. They can save time when making tarts and pies and give reliably good results.

Custard Fresh ready-made custard is great served hot as an accompaniment to desserts, but it also makes a useful base for ice creams, sauces and soufflés.

Frozen fruit Mixed frozen fruit has already been prepared, ready for making into desserts and sauces. It is available all year round, which means that you can enjoy the sweet taste of summer fruits during the winter when they are out of season. Frozen fruit is often cheaper than fresh.

Above: *Good quality fresh custards are widely available in most supermarkets and make an ideal base for many sweet dishes.*

Above: *Frozen summer berries are available all year round and make a handy alternative to fresh ones in most cooked dishes.*

Cake mixes With the simple addition of an egg and water, these easy-to-use mixes can be turned into a freshly baked cake in no time at all. Scattering the cake mixture with chopped nuts before baking, or sandwiching the cake with cream and fresh summer fruits once it has cooled can transform these simple mixes from an "emergency" storecupboard (pantry) item into a fabulous tea time treat or delicious dessert with almost no effort.

Batter mixes These are another useful "emergency" product. Simply combine with an egg and water and use to make pancakes for breakfast or dessert, or to coat food before deep-frying.

Pizza base mixes and bread mixes Whereas ready-baked pizza bases tend to be rather cardboard-like, these mixes are excellent and take very little effort to make.

Cakes and cookies Store-bought cakes and cookies can often be used as the base for simple desserts. Dark chocolate brownies can be combined with cream and macerated fruit to create a rich, indulgent dessert, or blended with milk and ice cream to make a decadent milkshake. Broken ginger cookies or sponge fingers can be used as the base for many creamy desserts.

Above: *Crisp ginger cookies can be roughly broken or finely crushed and used as the base for simple desserts such as trifle.*

Pasta sauces Both bottled and fresh pasta sauces are widely available in most supermarkets. Simple tomato and herb sauces are useful for tossing with pasta, spreading over a pizza base or as the base for a quick soup. Ready-made cheese sauces are also versatile – not only good for serving with pasta, but also for topping vegetable gratins, or combining with whisked egg whites and extra grated cheese to make a quick and simple soufflé.

Microwave rice mixes A fairly recent invention, these come in a variety of flavours, including mushroom and pilau. They are extremely useful as the base for quick rice dishes such as kedgeree.

Bags of mixed salad These save time selecting and preparing a variety of leaves. For maximum flavour, choose a bag that includes baby leaves and herbs.

Making the Basics

Having a few ready-made basics, such as stocks, pasta sauces and flavoured oils, can really help with everyday cooking. They can all be bought ready-made in the supermarket, but they are easy to make at home. Stocks take time to prepare, but they can be stored in the freezer for several months. Flavoured oils are easy to make and keep in the same way as ordinary oils so it's well worth having a few in the cupboard. All the basic sauces, dressings, marinades and flavoured creams in this section are simple to make and can be made fresh or in advance.

Flavoured oils

Good quality olive oil can be flavoured with herbs, spices and aromatics to make rich-tasting oils that are perfect for drizzling, making dressings and cooking. Make a couple of different flavoured oils and store in a cool, dark place.

Herb-infused oil Half-fill a jar with washed and dried fresh herbs such as rosemary or basil. Pour over olive oil to cover, then seal the jar and place in a cool, dark place for 3 days. Strain the herb-flavoured oil into a clean jar or bottle and discard the herbs.

Lemon oil Finely pare the rind from 1 lemon, place on kitchen paper, and leave to dry for 1 day. Add the dried rind to a bottle of olive oil and leave to infuse for up to 3 days. Strain the oil into a clean bottle and discard the rind.

Chilli oil Add several dried chillies to a bottle of olive oil and leave to infuse for about 2 weeks before using. If the flavour is not sufficiently pronounced, leave for another week. The chillies can be left in the bottle and give a very decorative effect.

Garlic oil Add several whole garlic cloves to a bottle of olive oil and leave to infuse for about 2 weeks before using. If the flavour is not sufficiently pronounced, leave the oil to infuse for another week, then strain the oil into a clean bottle and store in a cool, dark place.

Stock

You cannot beat the flavour of good home-made stock so it's worth making a large batch and freezing it. To freeze, pour the cooled stock into 600ml/1 pint/2^1/$_2$ cup containers and freeze for up to 2 months.

Chicken stock Put a 1.3kg/3lb chicken carcass into a large pan with 2 peeled and quartered onions, 2 halved carrots, 2 roughly chopped celery sticks, 1 bouquet garni, 1 peeled garlic clove and 5 black peppercorns. Pour in 1.2 litres/2 pints/5 cups cold water to cover the chicken and vegetables and bring to the boil. Reduce the heat, cover and simmer for 4–5 hours, regularly skimming off any scum from the surface. Strain the stock through a sieve lined with kitchen paper and leave to cool.

Beef stock Preheat the oven to 230°C/450°F/Gas 8. Put 1.8kg/4lb beef bones in a roasting pan and roast for 40 minutes, until browned, turning occasionally. Transfer the bones and vegetables to a large pan. Cover with water, add 2 chopped tomatoes and cook as for chicken stock.

Fish stock Put 2 chopped onions, 1.3kg/3lb fish bones and heads, 300ml/^{1}/$_2$ pint/1^1/$_4$ cups white wine, 5 black peppercorns and 1 bouquet garni in a large pan. Pour in 2 litres/3^1/$_2$ pints/9 cups water. Bring to the boil and simmer for 20 minutes, skimming often. Strain the stock.

Vegetable stock Put 900g/2lb chopped vegetables, including onions, leeks, tomatoes, carrots, parsnips and cabbage, in a large pan. Pour in 1.5 litres/2^1/$_2$ pints/ 6^1/$_4$ cups water. Bring to the boil and simmer for 30 minutes, then strain.

Marinades

These strong-tasting mixes are perfect for adding flavour to meat, poultry, fish and vegetables. Most ingredients should be left to marinate for at least 30 minutes.

Ginger and soy marinade This is perfect for use with chicken and beef. Peel and grate a 2.5cm/1in piece of fresh root ginger and peel and finely chop a large garlic clove. In a small bowl, whisk together 60ml/ 4 tbsp olive oil with 75ml/ 5 tbsp dark soy sauce. Season with freshly ground black pepper and stir in the ginger and garlic.

Rosemary and garlic marinade This is ideal for robust fish, lamb and chicken. Roughly chop the leaves from 3 fresh rosemary sprigs. Finely chop 2 garlic cloves and whisk together with the rosemary, 75ml/5 tbsp olive oil and the juice of 1 lemon.

Lemon grass and lime marinade Use with fish and chicken. Finely chop 1 lemon grass stalk. Whisk together the grated rind and juice of 1 lime with 75ml/5 tbsp olive oil, salt and black pepper and the lemon grass.

Red wine and bay marinade This is ideal for red meat, particularly tougher cuts. Whisk together 150ml/^{1}/4 pint/ ^{2}/3 cup red wine, 1 chopped garlic clove, 2 torn fresh bay leaves and 45ml/3 tbsp olive oil. Season with black pepper.

Below: Marinades containing red wine are particularly good for tenderizing tougher cuts of meat such as stewing steak.

Dressings

Freshly made dressings are delicious drizzled over salads but are also tasty served with cooked vegetables and simply cooked fish, meat and poultry. You can make these dressings a few hours in advance and store them in a sealed container in the refrigerator until ready to use. Give them a quick whisk before drizzling over the food.

Honey and wholegrain mustard dressing
Drizzle this sweet, peppery dressing over leafy salads, fish, chicken and red meat dishes or toss with warm new potatoes. Whisk together 15ml/1 tbsp wholegrain mustard, 30ml/2 tbsp white wine vinegar, 15ml/1 tbsp honey and 75ml/5 tbsp extra virgin olive oil and season with salt and ground black pepper.

Orange and tarragon dressing
Serve this fresh, tangy dressing with salads and grilled (broiled) fish. In a small bowl, whisk together the rind and juice of 1 large orange with 45ml/ 3 tbsp olive oil and 15ml/1 tbsp chopped fresh tarragon. Season with salt and plenty of freshly ground black pepper to taste.

Toasted coriander and cumin dressing
Drizzle this warm, spicy dressing over grilled chicken, lamb or beef. Heat a small frying pan and sprinkle in 15ml/1 tbsp each of coriander and cumin seeds. Dry-fry until the seeds release their aromas and start to pop, then crush the seeds using a mortar and pestle. Add 45ml/3 tbsp olive oil, whisk to combine, then leave to infuse for 20 minutes. Season with salt and freshly ground black pepper to taste.

Savoury sauces

Hot and cold savoury sauces lie at the heart of many dishes or can be the finishing touch that makes a meal – tomato sauce tossed with pasta, cheese sauce poured over a vegetable gratin, apple sauce to accompany pork, or a spoonful of mayonnaise with poached salmon. This section covers all the basic sauces: from tomato and pesto sauces to toss with pasta and rich, fruity sauces to serve with meat and poultry to creamy ones such as mayonnaise.

Easy tomato sauce

This versatile sauce can be tossed with pasta, used on a pizza base or served with chicken or fish. Heat 15ml/ 1 tbsp olive oil in a pan, add 1 chopped onion and fry for 3–4 minutes until soft. Add 1 chopped garlic clove and cook for about, 1 minute more. Pour in 400g/14oz chopped canned tomatoes and stir in 15ml/1 tbsp tomato purée (paste). Add 30ml/2 tbsp dried oregano and simmer for about 15 minutes, until thickened. Season with salt and pepper.

Mustard cheese sauce

Toss this rich, creamy sauce with pasta, or serve with boiled vegetables or baked white fish. Melt 25g/1oz/2 tbsp butter in a medium pan and stir in 25g/1oz/^{1}/4 cup plain (all-purpose) flour. Remove the pan from the heat and stir in 5ml/1 tsp prepared English mustard, then gradually add 200ml/7fl oz/scant 1 cup milk, stirring well to remove any lumps. (If the sauce becomes lumpy, whisk until smooth.) Return the pan to the heat and bring to the boil, stirring constantly. Remove from the heat and stir in 115g/4oz/ 1 cup grated Gruyère or Cheddar cheese. Season to taste with salt and freshly ground black pepper.

Quick satay sauce

Serve this spicy Asian-style sauce with grilled (broiled) chicken, beef or prawns, or toss with freshly cooked egg noodles. Put 30ml/ 2 tbsp crunchy peanut butter in a pan and stir in 150ml/^{1}/4 pint/^{2}/3 cup coconut milk, 45ml/3 tbsp hot water, a pinch of chilli powder and 30ml/2 tbsp light soy sauce. Heat gently and simmer for 1 minute.

Apple sauce Serve with pork. Peel, core and slice 450g/ 1lb cooking apples and place in a pan. Add a splash of water, 15ml/1 tbsp caster (superfine) sugar and a few whole cloves. Cook the apples over a gentle heat, stirring occasionally, until the fruit becomes pulpy.

Quick cranberry sauce Serve with roast chicken or turkey. Put 225g/8oz/2 cups cranberries in a pan with 75g/3oz/scant ^{1}/2 cup light muscovado sugar, 45ml/3 tbsp port and 45ml/3 tbsp orange juice. Bring to the boil, then simmer, uncovered, for 10 minutes, or until the cranberries are tender. Stir occasionally to stop the fruit from sticking.

Gooseberry relish Serve this tart relish with oily fish, such as mackerel, or fatty meat such as pork. Put 225g/ 8oz fresh or frozen gooseberries in a pan with 225g/8oz/ generous 1 cup caster (superfine) sugar and 1 star anise. Add a splash of water and a little white wine if desired. Bring to the boil and simmer, uncovered, for 10 minutes, stirring occasionally until the fruit is soft and pulpy.

Below: *Sauces made from tart fruit, such as cranberries, are excellent served with mild or fatty roast poultry and meat.*

Traditional pesto This classic Italian sauce is made with basil, garlic, pine nuts and Parmesan cheese but there are many variations. Toss with pasta, stir into mashed potatoes or plain boiled rice, or use to flavour sauces and dressings. Put 50g/2oz fresh basil leaves in a food processor and blend to a paste with 25g/1oz/$^{1}/_4$ cup toasted pine nuts and 2 peeled garlic cloves. With the motor still running, drizzle in 120ml/4fl oz/$^{1}/_2$ cup extra virgin olive oil until the mixture forms a paste. Spoon the pesto into a bowl and stir in 25g/1oz/$^{1}/_3$ cup freshly grated Parmesan cheese. Season to taste with salt and freshly ground black pepper.

Parsley and walnut pesto Put 50g/2oz fresh parsley leaves in a food processor and blend to a paste with 25g/1oz/$^{1}/_4$ cup walnuts and 2 peeled garlic cloves. With the motor still running, drizzle in 120ml/4fl oz/$^{1}/_2$ cup extra virgin olive oil until the mixture forms a paste. Spoon the pesto into a bowl and stir in 25g/1oz/$^{1}/_3$ cup freshly grated Parmesan cheese. Season to taste with salt and freshly ground black pepper.

Gravy

This classic sauce for roast poultry and meat is quick and easy to make. Remove the cooked poultry or meat from the roasting pan, transfer to a serving platter, cover with foil and leave to rest. Spoon off all but about 30ml/2 tbsp of the cooking fat and juices, leaving the sediment in the pan. Place the pan over a low heat and add a splash of white wine for poultry or red wine for meat, stirring in any sediment from the roasting pan. Stir in 30ml/2 tbsp plain (all-purpose) flour and mix to a paste. Remove from the heat and gradually pour in 450ml/$^{3}/_4$ pint/scant 2 cups stock. Return to the heat and stir over a medium heat until the gravy comes to the boil. Simmer for 2–3 minutes, until thickened. Adjust the seasoning and serve.

Rocket pesto Put 50g/2oz fresh rocket (arugula) leaves into a food processor and blend to a paste with 25g/1oz/$^{1}/_4$ cup toasted pine nuts and 2 peeled garlic cloves. With the motor still running, drizzle in 120ml/4fl oz/$^{1}/_2$ cup extra virgin olive oil until the mixture forms a paste. Spoon the pesto into a bowl and stir in 25g/1oz/$^{1}/_3$ cup freshly grated Parmesan cheese. Season to taste with salt and freshly ground black pepper.

Asian-style pesto Try this Asian version of Italian pesto tossed with freshly cooked egg noodles. Put 50g/2oz fresh coriander (cilantro) leaves into a food processor and add 25g/1oz/$^{1}/_4$ cup toasted pine nuts, 2 peeled garlic cloves and 1 roughly chopped, seeded red chilli. Blend until smooth. With the motor still running, drizzle in 120ml/4fl oz/$^{1}/_2$ cup extra virgin olive oil until the mixture forms a paste. Spoon the pesto into a bowl and season to taste with salt and freshly ground black pepper.

Mayonnaise Once you have made your own mayonnaise you will never want to buy it again. Put 2 egg yolks, 10ml/2 tsp lemon juice, 5ml/1 tsp Dijon mustard and some salt and ground black pepper in a food processor. Process briefly to combine, then, with the motor running, drizzle in about 350ml/12fl oz/1$^{1}/_2$ cups olive oil. The mayonnaise will become thick and pale. Scrape the mayonnaise into a bowl, taste and add more lemon juice and salt and pepper if necessary.

Aioli This classic French garlic mayonnaise is particularly good served with piping hot chips (French fries). Make the mayonnaise as described above, adding 2 peeled garlic cloves to the food processor with the egg yolks.

Lemon mayonnaise This zesty, creamy mayonnnaise complements cold poached fish perfectly. Make the mayonnaise as described above, adding the grated rind of 1 lemon to the food processor with the egg yolks.

Herb mayonnaise Make the plain mayonnaise as described above. Finely chop a handful of fresh herbs, such as basil, coriander (cilantro) and tarragon, then stir into the freshly made mayonnaise.

Savoury dips

These richly flavoured dips are delicious served with tortilla chips, crudités or small savoury crackers, but can also be served as an accompaniment to grilled (broiled) or poached chicken and fish. The creamy dips also make flavourful dressings for salads; you may need to thin them slightly with a squeeze of lemon juice or a little cold water.

Blue cheese dip This sharp, tangy mixture is best served with crunchy crudites. Put 200ml/ 7fl oz/scant 1 cup crème fraîche in a large bowl and add 115g/4oz/1 cup crumbled blue cheese such as stilton. Stir well until the mixture is smooth and creamy. Season with salt and freshly ground black pepper and fold in 30ml/2 tbsp chopped fresh chives.

Sour cream and chive dip This tasty dip is a classic combination and goes particularly well with crudités and savoury crackers. Put 200ml/ 7fl oz/scant 1 cup sour cream in a bowl and add 30ml/2 tbsp snipped fresh chives and a pinch of caster (superfine) sugar. Stir well to mix, then season with salt and plenty of freshly ground black pepper to taste.

Avocado and cumin salsa Serve this spicy Mexican-style salsa with tortilla chips; they're the perfect shape for scooping up the chunky salsa. Peel, stone (pit) and roughly chop 1 ripe avocado. Transfer to a bowl and gently stir in 1 finely chopped fresh red chilli, 15ml/1 tbsp toasted crushed cumin seeds, 1 chopped ripe tomato, the juice of 1 lime, 45ml/3 tbsp olive oil and 30ml/2 tbsp chopped fresh coriander (cilantro). Season and serve immediately.

Sweet sauces

These luscious sauces are perfect spooned over ice cream and can turn a store-bought dessert into an indulgent treat.

Chocolate fudge sauce Put 175ml/6fl oz/³/₄ cup double (heavy) cream in a small pan with 45ml/3 tbsp golden (light corn) syrup, 200g/7oz/scant 1 cup light muscovado (brown) sugar and a pinch of salt. Heat gently, stirring, until the sugar has dissolved. Add 75g/3oz/¹/₂ cup chopped plain (semisweet) chocolate and stir until melted. Simmer the sauce gently for about 20 minutes, stirring occasionally, until thickened. To keep warm until ready to use, pour into a heatproof bowl, cover and place over a pan of simmering water.

Toffee chocolate sauce Roughly chop 2 Mars bars (chocolate toffee bars) and put them in a pan with 300ml/ ¹/₂ pint/1¹/₄ cups double (heavy) cream. Stir over a gentle heat until the chocolate bars have melted.

Raspberry and vanilla sauce Scrape the seeds from a vanilla pod into a food processor. Add 200g/7oz/1 cup raspberries and 30ml/2 tbsp icing (confectioners') sugar. Process to a purée, adding a little water to thin, if necessary.

Below: *Blended fruit sauces are quick and simple to make and are great drizzled over ice cream and many other desserts.*

Flavoured creams

Cream is the perfect accompaniment for any dessert – whether it's a healthy fruit salad, a sumptuous plum tart or a warming baked apple. Flavoured creams are even better and can transform a tasty dessert into a truly luscious one. The ideas below are all incredibly simple and can be prepared in advance and stored in the refrigerator until you are ready to serve.

Rosemary and almond cream This fragrant cream has a lovely texture and is good served with fruit compotes, pies and tarts. Pour 300ml/^{1}/2 pint/ 1^1/4 cups double (heavy) cream into a pan and add 2 fresh rosemary sprigs. Heat the mixture until just about to boil, then remove the pan from the heat and leave the mixture to infuse for 20 minutes. Remove the rosemary from the pan and discard. Pour the cream into a bowl and chill until cold. Whip the cold cream into soft peaks and stir in 30ml/2 tbsp chopped toasted almonds.

Rum and cinnamon cream You can serve this versatile cream with most desserts. It goes particularly well with coffee, chocolate and fruit. Pour 300ml/^{1}/2 pint/1^1/4 cups double (heavy) cream into a pan and add 1 cinnamon stick. Heat the mixture until just about to boil, then remove the pan from the heat and leave to infuse for about 20 minutes. Strain the cream through a fine sieve and place in the refrigerator until cold. Whip the cold cream until it stands in soft peaks, then stir in 30ml/2 tbsp rum and 15ml/1 tbsp icing (confectioners') sugar.

Marsala Mascarpone This rich, creamy Italian cheese is perfect for serving with grilled (broiled) fruit, tarts and hot desserts. Spoon 200g/7oz/scant 1 cup Mascarpone into a large bowl and add 30ml/2 tbsp icing (confectioners') sugar and 45ml/3 tbsp Marsala (Italian sweet wine). Beat the mixture well until smooth and thoroughly combined.

Cardamom cream

Warm, spicy cardamom pods make a wonderfully subtle, aromatic cream that is delicious served with fruit salads, compôtes, tarts and pies. It goes particularly well with tropical fruits such as mango. Pour 300ml/ ^{1}/2 pint/1^1/4 cups double (heavy) cream into a pan and add 3 green cardamom pods. Heat the mixture gently until just about to boil, then remove the pan from the heat and leave to infuse for about 20 minutes. Strain the cream through a fine sieve and place in the refrigerator until cold. Whip the cold cream until it stands in soft peaks.

Praline cream

1 Put 115g/4oz/^{1}/2 cup sugar and 75ml/5 tbsp water in a small, heavy pan. Stir over a gentle heat until the sugar has dissolved, then boil (not stirring) until golden.

2 Remove from the heat and stir in 50g/2oz/ ^{1}/3 cup whole blanched almonds and tip on to a lightly oiled baking sheet. Leave until hard.

3 Break the hardened nut mixture into smaller pieces and put in a food processor. Process for about 1 minute until finely chopped.

4 In a large bowl, whip 300ml/^{1}/2 pint/1^1/4 cups double (heavy) cream into soft peaks, then stir in the praline and serve immediately.

Making Simple Accompaniments

When you've made a delicious main meal, you need to serve it with equally tasty accompaniments. The following section is full of simple, speedy ideas for fabulous side dishes – from creamy mashed potatoes, fragrant rice and spicy noodles to Italian-style polenta and simple, healthy vegetables.

Mashed potatoes

Potatoes go well with just about any main dish. They can be cooked simply – boiled, steamed, fried or baked – but they are even better mashed with milk and butter to make creamy mashed potatoes. To make even more enticing side dishes, try stirring in different flavourings.

Perfect mashed potatoes Peel 675g/1¹/₂lb floury potatoes and cut them into large chunks. Place in a pan of salted boiling water. Return to the boil, then simmer for 15–20 minutes, or until completely tender. Drain the potatoes and return to the pan. Leave over a low heat for a couple of minutes, shaking the pan to drive off any excess moisture. Take the pan off the heat and, using a potato masher, mash the potatoes until smooth. Beat in 45–60ml/3–4 tbsp warm milk and a large knob (pat) of butter, then season with salt and freshly ground black pepper to taste.

Pesto mash This is a simple way to dress up plain mashed potatoes. It gives them real bite and a lovely green-specked appearance. Make mashed potatoes as described above, then stir in 30ml/2 tbsp pesto sauce until thoroughly combined.

Mustard mash Make mashed potatoes as above, then stir in 15–30ml/1–2 tbsp wholegrain mustard.

Parmesan and parsley mash Make mashed potatoes as above, then stir in 30ml/2 tbsp freshly grated Parmesan and 15ml/1 tbsp chopped fresh flat-leaf parsley.

Apple and thyme mash Serve with pork. Make mashed potatoes as above. Heat 25g/1oz/2 tbsp butter in a pan and add 2 peeled, cored and sliced eating apples. Fry for 4–5 minutes, turning. Roughly mash, then fold into the potatoes, with 15ml/1 tbsp fresh thyme leaves.

Crushed potatoes

This chunky, modern version of mashed potatoes tastes delicious and can be flavoured in different ways.

Crushed potatoes with parsley and lemon Cook 675g/1¹/₂lb new potatoes in salted boiling water for 15–20 minutes, until tender. Drain the potatoes and crush roughly, using a fork. Stir in 30ml/2 tbsp extra virgin olive oil, the grated rind and juice of 1 lemon and 30ml/2 tbsp chopped fresh flat-leaf parsley. Season with freshly ground black pepper to taste.

Crushed potatoes with garlic and basil Cook 675g/1¹/₂lb new potatoes in a pan of boiling salted water for 15–20 minutes until tender. Drain and crush roughly, using the back of a fork. Stir in 30ml/2 tbsp extra virgin olive oil, 2 finely chopped garlic cloves and a handful of torn basil leaves until well combined, then season with ground black pepper to taste.

Crushed potatoes with pine nuts and Parmesan Cook 675g/1¹/₂lb new potatoes in boiling salted water for 15–20 minutes until tender. Drain and crush using a fork. Stir in 30ml/2 tbsp extra virgin olive oil, 30ml/2 tbsp grated Parmesan cheese and 30ml/2 tbsp toasted pine nuts.

Rice

This versatile grain is the staple in many diets around the world. It can be served simply – either boiled or steamed – or can be flavoured or stir-fried with different ingredients to make a tasty, exciting accompaniment to curries, stir-fries, stews and grilled (broiled) meat or fish.

Easy egg-fried rice

Cook 115g/4oz/generous ½ cup long-grain rice in a large pan of boiling water for 10–12 minutes, until tender. Drain well and refresh under cold running water. Spread out on a baking sheet and leave until completely cold. Heat 30ml/2 tbsp sunflower oil in a large frying pan and add 1 finely chopped garlic clove. Cook for 1 minute, then add the rice and stir-fry for 1 minute. Push the rice to the side of the pan and pour 1 beaten egg into the pan. Cook the egg until set, then break up with a fork and stir into the rice. Add a splash of soy sauce, and mix well.

Star anise and cinnamon rice Add 225g/8oz/ generous 1 cup basmati rice to a large pan of salted boiling water. Return to the boil, then reduce the heat and add a cinnamon stick and 2 star anise and simmer gently for 10–15 minutes, until the rice is tender. Drain well and remove the star anise and cinnamon before serving.

Coconut rice Put 225g/8oz/generous 1 cup basmati rice in a pan and pour in a 400ml/14oz can coconut milk. Cover with water, add some salt and bring to the boil. Simmer for 12 minutes, or until the rice is tender. Drain well and serve.

Coriander and spring onion rice

Cook 225g/8oz/generous 1 cup basmati rice in a large pan of salted boiling water for about 12 minutes, or until tender. Drain the rice well and return to the pan. Stir in 3 finely sliced spring onions (scallions) and 1 roughly chopped bunch of fresh coriander (cilantro) until well mixed, then serve immediately.

Noodles

There are many different types of noodles, all of which are quick to cook and make the perfect accompaniment to Chinese- and Asian-style stir-fries and curries. Serve them on their own, or toss them with a few simple flavourings. They can also be served cold as a simple salad.

Spicy peanut noodles

Cook a 250g/9oz packet of egg noodles according to the instructions on the packet, then drain. Heat 15ml/1 tbsp sunflower oil in a wok and add 30ml/2 tbsp crunchy peanut butter. Add a splash of cold water and a dash of soy sauce and stir the mixture over a gentle heat until thoroughly combined. Add the noodles to the pan and toss to coat in the peanut mixture. Sprinkle with fresh coriander (cilantro) to serve.

Chilli and spring onion noodles

Soak 115g/4oz flat rice noodles in cold water for 30 minutes, until softened. Drain well. Heat 30ml/2 tbsp olive oil in a wok or large frying pan. Add 2 finely chopped garlic cloves and 1 seeded and finely chopped red chilli and fry gently for 2 minutes. Slice a bunch of spring onions (scallions) and add to the pan. Cook for a minute or so, then stir in the rice noodles. Season with salt and freshly ground black pepper before serving.

Soy and sesame egg noodles

Cook a 250g/9oz packet of egg noodles according to the instructions on the packet. Drain well and tip the noodles into a large bowl. Drizzle over 30ml/2 tbsp dark soy sauce and 10ml/2 tsp sesame oil, then sprinkle over 15ml/1 tbsp toasted sesame seeds and toss well until thoroughly combined. Serve the noodles hot, or cold as a salad.

Polenta

This classic Italian dish made from cornmeal makes a delicious accompaniment to many dishes and is a useful alternative to the usual potatoes, bread or pasta. It can be served in two ways – either soft, or set and cut into wedges and grilled (broiled) or fried. Soft polenta is rather like mashed potatoes, while the grilled or fried variety has a much firmer texture and lovely crisp shell. Both types can be enjoyed plain, or flavoured with other ingredients such as cheese, herbs and spices. Traditional polenta requires lengthy boiling and constant attention during cooking, but the quick-cook varieties, which are widely available in most large supermarkets, give excellent results and are much simpler and quicker to prepare.

Soft polenta Cook 225g/8oz/2 cups quick-cook polenta according to the instructions on the packet. As soon as the polenta is cooked, stir in about 50g/2oz/¼ cup butter. Season with salt and black pepper to taste, then serve immediately.

Soft polenta with Parmesan and sage Cook 225g/8oz/2 cups quick-cook polenta according to the instructions on the packet. As soon as the polenta is cooked, stir in 115g/4oz/1⅓ cups freshly grated Parmesan cheese and a handful of chopped fresh sage. Stir in a large knob (pat) of butter and season with salt and freshly ground black pepper to taste before serving.

Soft polenta with Cheddar cheese and thyme

Cook 225g/8oz/2 cups quick-cook polenta according to the instructions on the packet. As soon as the polenta is cooked, stir in 50g/2oz/½ cups grated Chedar cheese and 30ml/2 tbsp chopped fresh thyme until thoroughly combined. Stir a large knob (pat) of butter into the cheesy polenta and season with salt and plenty of freshly ground black pepper to taste before serving.

Fried chilli polenta triangles Cook 225g/8oz/2 cups quick-cook polenta according to the instructions on the packet. Stir in 5ml/1 tsp dried chilli flakes, check the seasoning, adding more if necessary, and spread the mixture out on an oiled baking sheet to a thickness of about 1cm/½in. Leave the polenta until cold and completely set, then chill for about 20 minutes. Turn the polenta out on to a board and cut it into large squares, then cut each square into 2 triangles. Heat 30ml/2 tbsp olive oil in a large frying pan. Fry the triangles in the olive oil for 2–3 minutes on each side, until golden, then lift out and briefly drain on kitchen paper before serving.

Grilled polenta with Gorgonzola Cook 225g/8oz/2 cups quick-cook polenta according to the instructions on the packet. Check the seasoning, adding more if necessary, and spread the mixture out on an oiled baking sheet to a thickness of about 1cm/½in. Leave the polenta until cold and completely set, then chill for about 20 minutes. Turn the polenta out on to a board and cut it into large squares, then cut each square into 2 triangles. Pre-heat the grill (broiler) and arrange the polenta triangles on the grill pan. Cook for about 5 minutes, or until golden brown, then turn over and top each triangle with a sliver of Gorgonzola. Grill for a further 5 minutes, or until bubbling.

Below: Wedges of set polenta are great fried and served as an accompaniment to stews, casseroles and other main dishes.

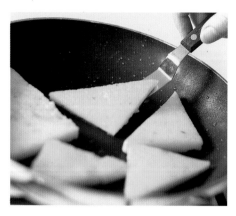

Quick and simple vegetables

Fresh vegetables are an essential part of your everyday diet. They are delicious cooked on their own but they can also be stir-fried with other ingredients. This can be an interesting way of adding flavour and creating colourful, enticing and heathy vegetable dishes.

Stir-fried cabbage with hazelnuts Heat 30ml/2 tbsp sunflower oil in a wok or large frying pan and add 4 roughly chopped rashers (strips) smoked streaky (fatty) bacon. Stir-fry for about 3 minutes, until the bacon starts to turn golden, then add $^1/_2$ shredded green cabbage to the pan. Stir-fry for 3–4 minutes, until the cabbage is just tender. Season with salt and freshly ground black pepper, and stir in 25g/1oz/ $^1/_4$ cup roughly chopped toasted hazelnuts.

Creamy stir-fried Brussels sprouts Heat 15ml/1 tbsp sunflower oil in a wok or large frying pan. Add 1 chopped garlic clove and stir-fry for about 30 seconds. Shred 450g/ 1lb Brussels sprouts and add to the pan. Stir-fry for 3–4 minutes, until just tender. Season with salt and pepper and stir in 30ml/2 tbsp crème fraîche. Warm through for 1 minute before serving.

Honey-fried parsnips and celeriac Peel 250g/ 8oz parsnips and 115g/ 4oz celeriac. Cut both into matchsticks. Heat 30ml/ 2 tbsp olive oil in a wok or large frying pan and add the parsnips and celeriac. Fry over a gentle heat for 6–7 minutes, stirring occasionally, until golden and tender. Season with salt and ground black pepper and stir in 15ml/1 tbsp clear honey. Allow to bubble for 1 minute before serving.

Flavoured breads

Bread makes a simple accompaniment to many meals and is the perfect ready-made side dish when time is short. Look out for part-baked breads that you can finish off in the oven, so you can enjoy the taste of freshly baked bread in a few minutes.

Ciabatta This chewy Italian bread is long and oval in shape and is commonly available in ready-to-bake form. Look out for ciabatta with added sun-dried tomatoes or olives.

Focaccia This flat, dimpled Italian bread is made with olive oil and has a softer texture than ciabatta. It is available plain but is also often flavoured with fresh rosemary and garlic.

Naan Traditionally cooked in a clay oven, this Indian bread is easy to find in supermarkets and makes a tasty accompaniment to curries. It is available plain, and also flavoured with spices.

Chapati This Indian flatbread is less heavy than naan and makes a good alternative. The small, round breads can be a little more difficult to find but are worth searching for.

Above: *Rosemary focaccia has a crumbly texture and is perfect for sandwiches and serving with Italian dishes.*

Planning a Menu

Getting together with friends and family to enjoy good food is one of life's most enjoyable experiences. There's nothing better than inviting friends over to enjoy a leisurely lunch, relaxing dinner or summer barbecue and making sure that everyone has a great time. But just because you are the host, it doesn't mean that you can't enjoy yourself too. Cooking and entertaining should be fun for everybody – including the cook. Try following the suggestions below to ensure your party goes smoothly and that you enjoy the occasion as much as your guests. The key to success is always to plan ahead.

- Make a list of the people you have invited and work out how many you need to cater for. Remember to check if anyone is vegetarian or has special dietary requirements such as an allergy to nuts or dairy products.

- Decide what you are going to make, then make sure you have all the equipment you need. If necessary, buy or borrow the items from a friend. When planning the menu, choose dishes you can cook with confidence and avoid being too adventurous. There's no point in cooking to impress if you can't pull it off.

- Ensure you have enough space in the refrigerator for drinks, ingredients and dishes that need to be chilled. If necessary, have a clear-out and remove any unnecessary items to make space.

- Don't leave shopping for ingredients to the last minute. Buy everything you need the day before. This gives you plenty of time for preparation, and also gives you time to track down ingredients elsewhere if the supermarket or food store is out of stock.

- Try to prepare as much as you can in advance. If some dishes can be made, or part-prepared the day before, then it's well worth doing.

- On the day, don't leave everything to the last minute. Prepare in good time, leaving yourself time to relax before your guests arrive.

Healthy breakfast

This healthy breakfast is the perfect way to give your system a boost. It's low in fat, packed with health-giving vitamins and nutrients and offers slow-release energy to keep you going throughout the morning.

Beetroot, ginger and orange juice
This refreshing blend of juices is full of vitamins and nutrients to cleanse and boost the system. Make sure you drink the juice as soon as you've made it because the vitamin content will begin to deplete soon after making.

Zingy papaya, lime and ginger salad
A refreshing fruit salad is the perfect way to start your day. Papaya and ginger are beneficial for the digestion and the tangy flavours of ginger and lime will wake you up with a zing.

Cranachan
The oats in this creamy breakfast dish are packed with slow-release carbohydrates that will sustain you until lunchtime. If you want to be really healthy, use low-fat Greek (US strained plain) yogurt.

Indulgent breakfast

This fabulous combination of dishes is perfect for a lazy weekend breakfast or brunch. You can even prepare the apricot turnovers the night before so you can really take it easy and just enjoy.

Cardamom hot chocolate
This rich, spiced hot chocolate is the perfect way to start a lazy weekend morning. It's particularly good in winter when you want something piping hot.

Apricot turnovers
Make these the night before and keep them in the refrigerator to bake in the morning. If you prefer, you can use rhubarb or raspberry compote in place of apricot.

Smoked salmon and chive omelette
Smoked salmon is a real treat for breakfast and you can buy small packets of smoked salmon quite cheaply. If you don't like fish, try serving Eggs Benedict instead.

Supper for two

For an intimate dinner for two, keep the tone informal. Prepare as much as you can in advance
so that you can relax and enjoy your friend's company when he or she arrives.

Potted shrimps with cayenne pepper
These can be made the day before and kept in the refrigerator – but remember to order fresh shrimps from your fishmonger.

Crème fraîche and coriander chicken
Delicious and quick so your guest will not sit alone while you are cooking!

Green salad
Choose a mixed bag of leaves with plenty of herbs for extra flavour. Whether you dress it or not is up to you.

Grilled pineapple and rum cream
This luscious dessert can be made ahead and kept in the refrigerator until ready to serve.

Formal entertaining

Although you're taking a more formal approach, it doesn't mean you can't enjoy yourself. To get the party going,
serve a tasty aperitif, such as Quick Bloody Mary, when your guests arrive.

Chicken liver and brandy pâté
This simple appetizer is best made the day before to allow its flavours to develop. Serve with crusty bread or Melba toast.

Sea bass with parsley and lime butter
Remember to order the fish to avoid disappointment and last-minute panic. Ask the fishmonger to fillet and scale it for you.

Green beans with almond and lemon butter
Lightly cook the beans in advance, then warm them through with the almond butter at the last minute.

Crushed potatoes with parsley and lemon

Roast peaches with amaretto
These peaches make the perfect end to a meal. For the more daring cook, try making passion fruit soufflés.
They need to be made at the last minute, but you can prepare the ramekin dishes in advance.

Barbecue for 12

When the weather is good, it is fun to go outdoors and cook over the coals. Make everything in advance and keep it in the refrigerator, ready to be cooked on the grill. Serve salads in bowls and let everyone help themselves.

Barbecued sardines with orange and parsley
Ask your fishmonger to get you the freshest sardines possible. Even people who don't think they like sardines will adore these!

Cumin- and coriander-rubbed lamb
Prepare the lamb several hours ahead to let the flavours develop. Let the coals get hot before putting the lamb on the barbecue.

Spring onion flatbreads
These can be made ahead of time if you prefer and served warm or at room temperature.

Roast aubergines with feta and coriander
These are perfect for vegetarian guests but they will also be a hit with meat eaters. You can use different types of cheese such as goat's cheese or halloumi if you prefer.

Potato and caraway seed salad
A potato salad is a barbecue must – caraway seeds give this one a slight edge.

Butter bean, tomato and red onion salad
This is quite a substantial salad, so serve a leafy mix as well. Toss everything together in advance and leave the flavours to develop.

Cuba Libre
Make a big jug with plenty of ice – but remember to offer soft drinks too.

Sunday lunch

This is probably one of the most relaxed and informal meals of the week and is surprisingly easy to make.
Get everyone to help out in the kitchen to make it more relaxing for you.

Roast chicken with black pudding and sage
Nobody will expect the surprise black pudding stuffing, but it is so delicious they will be back for second helpings.
If you have invited a lot of guests, you will need to roast two chickens.

Crisp and golden roast potatoes with goose fat and garlic
Sunday lunch is not Sunday lunch without roast potatoes. Remember to fluff up the outside of the potatoes
when you drain them to get a really crispy result.

Cheesy creamy leeks
These make a tasty alternative to plain boiled or steamed vegetables. Use sliced large leeks, or whole baby ones.

Plum and almond tart
This impressive tart is easy to make and can be prepared in advance. Serve it warm with generous dollops of clotted cream.

Picnic

Picnics are great fun. Take lots of paper napkins, plates, plastic cups and cutlery. A cool box is invaluable for transporting food and keeping it fresh so if you don't have one, try to borrow one from a friend.

Artichoke and cumin dip
Take this tasty dip in a plastic container and pack breadsticks and raw vegetable crudités for dipping.

Cannellini bean pâté
Serve this as a second dip or spread on wedges of fresh soda bread. Alternatively, use it as a sandwich filling with slices of fresh tomato.

Marinated feta with lemon and oregano
Make this the day before and transport it in a container with a well-fitting lid.

Traditional Irish soda bread
This delicious bread is superb with the feta and the cannellini bean pâté. If you have time, make it on the morning of the picnic.

Pasta with fresh tomatoes and basil
Use small pasta shapes, which are easier to eat. Take a small bottle of olive oil so that you can add an extra drizzle before serving.

Blueberry cake
To make serving easier, cut the cake into wedges before you go, and take along a pot of cream or crème fraîche to serve with it.

Summer *al fresco* lunch

Al fresco simply means outdoors – and there are few things so enjoyable as eating outside when the sun is shining.

Peperonata
Make this the night before to allow the flavours to develop, and serve with bread and olives.

Fresh crab sandwiches
Little preparation is needed for these glorious sandwiches – but do remember to order the crabs from the fishmonger.

Halloumi and fennel salad
This richly flavoured salad is the perfect partner for crab sandwiches and is ideal if you have the barbecue out.

Watermelon ice
This refreshing, fruity dessert is the perfect way to round off a summer lunch.

Breakfasts and Brunches

NO ONE WANTS THE BOTHER OF LOTS OF INGREDIENTS
AND LENGTHY PREPARATION FOR THEIR FIRST MEAL OF
THE DAY. THIS COLLECTION OF WONDERFULLY SIMPLE,
YET DELICIOUS DISHES HAS BEEN CREATED WITH THAT
IN MIND. WHETHER YOU WANT A HEALTHY, VITAMIN-
PACKED FRUIT SALAD FOR BREAKFAST OR AN
INDULGENT SERVING OF EGGS BENEDICT FOR A LAZY
WEEKEND BRUNCH, YOU'RE SURE TO FIND THE
PERFECT RECIPE TO SET YOU UP FOR THE DAY.

Zingy Papaya, Lime and Ginger Salad

This refreshing, fruity salad makes a lovely light breakfast, perfect for the summer months. Choose really ripe, fragrant papayas for the best flavour.

SERVES FOUR

1 Cut the papaya in half lengthways and scoop out the seeds, using a teaspoon. Using a sharp knife, cut the flesh into thin slices and arrange on a platter.

2 Squeeze the lime juice over the papaya and sprinkle with the sliced stem ginger. Serve immediately.

2 large ripe papayas

juice of 1 fresh lime

2 pieces preserved stem ginger, finely sliced

VARIATION *This refreshing fruit salad is delicious made with other tropical fruit. Try using 2 ripe peeled stoned mangoes in place of the papayas.*

Cantaloupe Melon with Grilled Strawberries

If strawberries are slightly underripe, sprinkling them with a little sugar and grilling them will help bring out their flavour.

SERVES FOUR

1 Preheat the grill (broiler) to high. Hull the strawberries and cut them in half. Arrange the fruit in a single layer, cut side up, on a baking sheet or in an ovenproof dish and dust with the icing sugar.

2 Grill (broil) the strawberries for 4–5 minutes, or until the sugar starts to bubble and turn golden.

3 Meanwhile, scoop out the seeds from the half melon using a spoon. Using a sharp knife, remove the skin, then cut the flesh into wedges and arrange on a serving plate with the grilled strawberries. Serve immediately.

115g/4oz/1 cup strawberries

15ml/1 tbsp icing (confectioners') sugar

$^1/_2$ cantaloupe melon

Crunchy Oat Cereal

Serve this tasty crunchy cereal simply with milk or, for a real treat, with yogurt and fresh fruit such as raspberries or blueberries.

SERVES SIX

1 Preheat oven to 160°C/325°F/Gas 3. Mix all the ingredients together and spread on to a large baking tray.

2 Bake for 30–35 minutes, or until golden and crunchy. Leave to cool, then break up into clumps and serve.

200g/7oz/1³⁄₄ cups jumbo rolled oats

150g/5oz/1¹⁄₄ cups pecan nuts, roughly chopped

90ml/6 tbsp maple syrup

FROM THE STORECUPBOARD

75g/3oz/6 tbsp butter, melted

COOK'S TIPS
• This crunchy oat cereal will keep in an airtight container for up to two weeks. Store in a cool, dry place.
• You can use other types of nuts if you prefer. Try roughly chopped almonds or hazelnuts instead of pecan nuts, or use a mixture.

Cranachan

This lovely, nutritious breakfast dish is a traditional Scottish recipe, and is delicious served with a generous drizzle of heather honey. It is also absolutely wonderful served with fresh blueberries or blackberries in place of the raspberries.

SERVES FOUR

75g/3oz crunchy oat cereal

600ml/1 pint/2¹/₂ cups Greek (strained plain) yogurt

250g/9oz/1¹/₃ cups raspberries

1 Preheat the grill (broiler) to high. Spread the oat cereal on a baking sheet and place under the hot grill for 3–4 minutes, stirring regularly. Set aside to cool.

2 When the cereal has cooled completely, fold it into the Greek yogurt, then gently fold in 200g/7oz/generous 1 cup of the raspberries, being careful not to crush the berries too much.

3 Spoon the yogurt mixture into four serving glasses or dishes, top with the remaining raspberries and serve immediately.

Chocolate Brioche Sandwiches

This luxury breakfast sandwich is a bit of a twist on the classic *pain au chocolat* and beats a boring slice of toast any day. The pale green pistachio nuts work really well with the chocolate spread, adding a satisfying crunch as well as a lovely contrast in colour.

SERVES FOUR

1 Toast the brioche slices until golden on both sides. Spread four of the slices thickly with the chocolate spread and sprinkle over the chopped pistachio nuts in an even layer.

2 Place the remaining brioche slices on top of the chocolate and nuts and press down gently. Using a sharp knife, cut the sandwiches in half diagonally and serve immediately.

8 thick brioche
bread slices

120ml/8 tbsp
chocolate spread

30ml/2 tbsp shelled
pistachio nuts, finely
chopped

COOK'S TIP

Brioche is a classic butter-enriched bread from France. It has a wonderful golden colour and slightly sweet taste. It is available in most supermarkets but you can use ordinary white bread if you can't get hold of brioche. Use an uncut loaf rather than a pre-sliced one so that you can cut thick slices.

Roast Bananas with Greek Yogurt and Honey

Roasting bananas like this brings out their natural sweetness. If you are watching the calories, use low-fat Greek yogurt and omit the nuts. Use ripe bananas for maximum flavour. You can also cook bananas in this way over a barbecue and serve them as a simple barbecue dessert drizzled with a little honey.

SERVES FOUR

2 ripe bananas, peeled

500ml/17fl oz/2¼ cups
Greek (US strained plain)
yogurt with honey

30ml/2 tbsp toasted
hazelnuts, roughly
chopped

1 Preheat the oven to 200°C/400°F Gas 6. Wrap the bananas in foil and bake for 20 minutes. Leave the bananas to cool completely, then unwrap, place in a small bowl and mash roughly with a fork.

2 Pour the yogurt into a large bowl, add the mashed bananas and gently fold them into the yogurt. Sprinkle with the hazelnuts and serve.

Apricot Turnovers

These sweet and succulent pastries are delicious served with a big cup of milky coffee for a late breakfast or mid-morning treat.

SERVES FOUR

1 Preheat the oven to 190°C/375°F/Gas 5. Roll out the pastry on a lightly floured surface to a 25cm/10in square. Using a sharp knife, cut the pastry into four 13cm/5in squares.

2 Place a tablespoon of the apricot conserve in the middle of each square of pastry. Using a pastry brush, brush the edges of the pastry with a little cold water and fold each square over to form a triangle. Gently press the edges together to seal.

3 Carefully transfer the turnovers to a baking sheet and bake for 15–20 minutes, or until risen and golden. Using a metal spatula, remove the pastries to a wire rack to cool, then dust generously with icing sugar and serve.

225g/8oz ready-made puff pastry, thawed if frozen

60ml/4 tbsp apricot conserve

30ml/2 tbsp icing (confectioners') sugar

Warm Pancakes with Caramelized Pears

If you can find them, use Williams pears for this recipe because they are juicier than most other varieties. For a really indulgent breakfast, top with a generous spoonful of crème fraîche or fromage frais.

SERVES FOUR

8 ready-made pancakes

4 ripe pears, peeled, cored and thickly sliced

30ml/2 tbsp light muscovado (brown) sugar

FROM THE STORECUPBOARD

50g/2oz/¹/₄ cup butter

1 Preheat the oven to 150°C/330°F/Gas 2. Tightly wrap the pancakes in foil and place in the oven to warm through.

2 Meanwhile, heat the butter in a large frying pan and add the pears. Fry for 2–3 minutes, until the undersides are golden. Turn the pears over and sprinkle with sugar. Cook for a further 2–3 minutes, or until the sugar dissolves and the pan juices become sticky.

3 Remove the pancakes from the oven and take them out of the foil. Divide the pears among the pancakes, placing them in one quarter. Fold each pancake in half over the filling, then into quarters and place two folded pancakes on each plate. Drizzle over any remaining juices and serve immediately.

Eggy Bread Panettone

Thickly sliced stale white bread is usually used for eggy bread, but the slightly dry texture of panettone makes a great alternative. Serve with a selection of fresh summer fruits such as strawberries, raspberries and blackcurrants.

SERVES FOUR

1 Break the eggs into a bowl and beat with a fork, then tip them into a shallow dish. Dip the panettone slices in the beaten egg, turning them to coat evenly.

2 Heat the butter or oil in a large non-stick frying pan and add the panettone slices. (You will probably have to do this in batches, depending on the size of the pan.) Fry the panettone slices over a medium heat for 2–3 minutes on each side, until golden brown.

3 Remove the panettone slices from the pan and drain on kitchen paper. Cut the slices in half diagonally and dust with the sugar. Serve immediately.

2 large (US extra large) eggs

4 large panettone slices

30ml/2 tbsp caster (superfine) sugar

FROM THE STORECUPBOARD

50g/2oz/$^1/_4$ cup butter or 30ml/2 tbsp sunflower oil

Scotch Pancakes with Bacon and Maple Syrup

Also known as drop scones, Scotch pancakes are available in most supermarkets. Raisin varieties also work well in this recipe.

SERVES FOUR

8 ready-made Scotch pancakes

8 dry-cured smoked back (lean) bacon rashers (strips)

30ml/2 tbsp maple syrup

1 Preheat the oven to 150°C/330°F/Gas 2. Wrap the pancakes in a sheet of foil and place them in the oven to warm through.

2 Meanwhile, preheat the grill (broiler) and arrange the bacon on a grill pan. Grill (broil) for 3–4 minutes on each side, until crisp.

3 Divide the warmed pancakes between four warmed serving plates and top with the grilled bacon rashers. Drizzle with the maple syrup and serve immediately.

Croque-monsieur

This classic French toastie is delicious served at any time of day, but with a foaming cup of milky coffee it makes a particularly enjoyable brunch dish. Gruyère is traditionally used, but you could use mild Cheddar instead. Prosciutto and Gorgonzola, served with a smear of mustard, also make a fabulous alternative to the classic ham and Gruyère combination.

SERVES FOUR

8 white bread slices

4 large lean ham slices

175g/6oz Gruyère cheese, thinly sliced

FROM THE STORECUPBOARD

a little softened butter

ground black pepper

1 Preheat the grill (broiler). Arrange the bread on the grill rack and toast four slices on both sides and the other four slices on one side only.

2 Butter the slices of bread that have been toasted on both sides and top with the ham, then the cheese, and season with plenty of ground black pepper.

3 Lay the remaining, half-toasted bread slices on top of the cheese, with the untoasted side uppermost. Grill the tops of the sandwiches until golden brown, then cut them in half using a sharp knife and serve immediately.

Eggs Benedict

Use a good quality bought hollandaise sauce for this recipe because it will make all the difference to the end result. Eggs Benedict are delicious served on half a toasted English muffin. Always use organic eggs – they have a superior flavour to eggs from battery hens.

SERVES FOUR

1 Pour cold water into a medium pan to a depth of about 5cm/2in and bring to a gentle simmer. Crack two eggs into the pan and bring back to the simmer. Simmer for 2–3 minutes, until the white is set, but the yolk is still soft.

2 Meanwhile, arrange the ham slices on four serving plates (or on top of four toasted, buttered muffin halves if using). Remove the eggs from the pan using a slotted spoon and place on top of the ham on two of the plates. Cook the remaining eggs in the same way.

3 Spoon the hollandaise sauce over the eggs, sprinkle with salt and pepper and serve immediately.

4 large (US extra large) eggs

4 lean ham slices

60ml/4 tbsp hollandaise sauce

FROM THE STORECUPBOARD

salt and ground black pepper

VARIATION If you prefer eggs cooked all the way through, scramble them instead of poaching. Then spoon over the ham and top with hollandaise sauce as before.

Smoked Salmon and Chive Omelette

The addition of a generous portion of chopped smoked salmon gives a really luxurious finish to this simple, classic dish. You can use this omelette recipe as the basis of endless variations. Simply replace the salmon and chives with other ingredients such as chopped ham and parsley or grated Cheddar and torn basil leaves.

SERVES TWO

1 Beat the eggs until just combined, then stir in the chives and season with salt and pepper.

2 Heat the butter in a medium-sized frying pan until foamy. Pour in the eggs and cook over a medium heat for 3–4 minutes, drawing the cooked egg from around the edge into the centre of the pan from time to time.

3 At this stage, you can either leave the top of the omelette slightly soft or finish it off under the grill (broiler), depending on how you like your omelette. Top with the smoked salmon, fold the omelette over and cut in half to serve.

4 eggs

15ml/1 tbsp chopped fresh chives

50g/2oz smoked salmon, roughly chopped

FROM THE STORECUPBOARD

a knob (pat) of butter

salt and ground black pepper

Quick Kedgeree

Kedgeree is a rice, lentil and onion dish that originally came from India. Fish and eggs were added by the British to make the breakfast dish we know and love today. A garnish of fresh coriander (cilantro) leaves adds extra flavour and colour.

SERVES FOUR

175g/6oz undyed smoked haddock fillet

4 eggs

2 × 250g/9oz packets microwave pilau rice

FROM THE STORECUPBOARD

salt and ground black pepper

1 Preheat the grill (broiler) to medium. Place the smoked haddock on a baking sheet and grill for about 10 minutes, or until cooked through.

2 Meanwhile, place the eggs in a pan of cold water and bring to the boil. Cook for 6–7 minutes, then drain and place under cold running water until cool enough to handle.

3 While the eggs and haddock are cooking, cook the rice according to the instructions on the packet. Shell the eggs and cut into halves or quarters. Flake the fish and gently mix into the rice, with the eggs, taking care not to break up the eggs too much. Spoon onto serving plates, and serve immediately.

Snacks and Appetizers

WHEN YOU WANT A SNACK, OR A LITTLE SOMETHING
TO WHET THE APPETITE BEFORE A MAIN MEAL – THINK
SIMPLICITY. FROM MOUTHWATERING DIPS TO SPICY
PRAWN SKEWERS AND CRISPY SAMOSAS, THIS CHAPTER
IS PACKED WITH SIMPLE, FUSS-FREE IDEAS THAT YOU
WON'T BE ABLE TO RESIST. SERVE GOLDEN, MELT-IN-
THE-MOUTH PARMESAN TUILES OR GOLDEN GRUYÈRE
AND BASIL TORTILLAS WITH DRINKS, OR ENJOY CRAB
AND WATER-CHESTNUT WONTONS AS AN APPETIZER.

Spanish Salted Almonds

Served with a glass of chilled dry sherry, these delicious salted nuts make a perfect tapas dish or pre-dinner snack.

SERVES FOUR TO SIX

1 Preheat the oven 200°C/400°F/Gas 6. Whisk the egg white in a bowl until it forms stiff peaks.

2 Add the almonds to the egg white, and stir until the nuts are thoroughly coated. Tip the mixture on to a baking sheet and spread out evenly in a single layer.

3 Sprinkle the salt over the almonds and bake for about 15 minutes, or until the egg white and salt are crusty. Leave to cool completely, then serve in bowls with a selection of other nibbles, dips and pâtés.

1 egg white

200g/7oz/generous 1 cup shelled unblanched almonds

a good handful of flaked sea salt

Golden Gruyère and Basil Tortillas

These simple fried tortilla wedges make a great late-night snack with sweet chilli sauce. If you have a few slices of ham or salami in the refrigerator, add these to the tortillas as well.

SERVES TWO

1 Heat the oil in a frying pan, over a medium heat. Add one of the tortillas, arrange the Gruyère cheese slices and basil leaves on top and season with salt and pepper.

2 Place the remaining tortilla on top to make a sandwich and flip the whole thing over with a metal spatula. Cook for a few minutes, until the underneath is golden.

3 Slide the tortilla sandwich on to a chopping board or plate and cut into wedges. Serve immediately.

2 soft flour tortillas

115g/4oz Gruyère cheese, thinly sliced

a handful of fresh basil leaves

FROM THE STORECUPBOARD

15ml/1 tbsp olive oil

salt and ground black pepper

Polenta Chips

These tasty Parmesan-flavoured batons are best served warm from the oven with a spicy, tangy dip. A bowl of Thai chilli dipping sauce or a creamy, chilli-spiked guacamole are perfect for dipping into.

MAKES ABOUT EIGHTY

1 Put 1.5 litres/2½ pints/6¼ cups water into a large heavy pan and bring to the boil. Reduce the heat, add the salt and pour in the polenta in a steady stream, stirring constantly with a wooden spoon. Cook over a low heat for about 5 minutes, stirring, until the mixture thickens and comes away from the sides of the pan.

2 Remove the pan from the heat and add the cheese and butter. Season to taste. Stir well until the mixture is smooth. Pour on to a smooth surface, such as a marble slab or a baking sheet.

3 Using a metal spatula, spread out the polenta to a thickness of 2cm/¾in and shape into a rectangle. Leave to stand for at least 30 minutes until cold. Meanwhile preheat the oven to 200°C/400°F/Gas 6 and lightly oil two or three baking sheets.

4 Cut the polenta slab in half, then carefully cut into even-size strips. Bake for 40–50 minutes, or until dark golden brown and crunchy, turning from time to time. Serve warm.

375g/13oz/3¼ cups instant polenta

150g/5oz/1½ cups freshly grated Parmesan cheese

FROM THE STORECUPBOARD

10ml/2 tsp salt, plus extra

90g/3½oz/7 tbsp butter

10ml/2 tsp cracked black pepper

olive oil, for brushing

Parmesan Tuiles

These lacy tuiles look very impressive and make splendid nibbles for a party, but they couldn't be easier to make. Believe or not, they use only a single ingredient – Parmesan cheese.

MAKES EIGHT TO TEN

1 Preheat the oven to 200°C/400°F/Gas 6. Line two baking sheets with baking parchment. Grate the cheese using a fine grater, pulling it down slowly to make long strands.

2 Spread the grated cheese in 7.5–9cm/3–3½in rounds on the baking parchment, forking it into shape. Do not spread the cheese too thickly; it should just cover the parchment. Bake for 5–7 minutes, or until bubbling and golden brown.

3 Leave the tuiles on the baking sheet for about 30 seconds and then carefully transfer, using a metal spatula, to a wire rack to cool completely. Alternatively, drape over a rolling pin to make a curved shape.

115g/4oz Parmesan cheese

COOK'S TIP
Tuiles can be made into little cup shapes by draping over an upturned egg cup. These little cups can be filled to make tasty treats to serve with drinks. Try a little cream cheese flavoured with herbs.

Peperonata

This richly flavoured spicy tomato and sweet red pepper dip is delicious served with crisp Italian-style bread sticks – enjoy it with drinks or as a snack while watching television. It also makes a tasty relish served with grilled chicken and fish dishes. It is delicious served either hot, cold or at room temperature and can be stored in the refrigerator for several days.

SERVES FOUR

1 Heat the oil in a large pan over a low heat and add the sliced peppers. Cook very gently, stirring occasionally for 3–4 minutes.

2 Add the chilli flakes to the pan and cook for 1 minute, then pour in the tomatoes and season. Cook gently for 50 minutes to 1 hour, stirring occasionally.

COOK'S TIP *Long, slow cooking helps to bring out the sweetness of the peppers and tomatoes, so don't be tempted to cheat on the cooking time by cooking over a higher heat.*

2 large red (bell) peppers, halved, seeded and sliced

pinch dried chilli flakes

400g/14oz can pomodorino tomatoes

FROM THE STORECUPBOARD

60ml/4 tbsp garlic-infused olive oil

salt and ground black pepper

Artichoke and Cumin Dip

This dip is so easy to make and is unbelievably tasty. Serve with olives, hummus and wedges of pitta bread to make a summery snack selection. Grilled artichokes bottled in oil have a fabulous flavour and can be used instead of canned artichokes. You can also vary the flavourings – try adding chilli powder in place of the cumin and add a handful of basil leaves to the artichokes before blending.

SERVES FOUR

1 Put the artichoke hearts in a food processor with the garlic and ground cumin, and a generous drizzle of olive oil. Process to a smooth purée and season with plenty of salt and ground black pepper to taste.

2 Spoon the purée into a serving bowl and serve with an extra drizzle of olive oil swirled on the top and slices of warm pitta bread for dipping.

2 x 400g/14oz cans artichoke hearts, drained

2 garlic cloves, peeled

2.5ml/½ tsp ground cumin

FROM THE STORECUPBOARD

olive oil

salt and ground black pepper

Cannellini Bean Pâté

Serve this simple pâté with melba toast or toasted wholegrain bread as an appetizer or snack. A dusting of paprika gives an extra kick. You can also use other types of canned beans such as kidney beans.

SERVES FOUR

2 x 400g/14oz cans cannellini beans, drained and rinsed

50g/2oz mature Cheddar cheese, finely grated

30ml/2 tbsp chopped fresh parsley

FROM THE STORECUPBOARD

45ml/3 tbsp olive oil

salt and ground black pepper

1 Put the cannellini beans in a food processor with the olive oil, and process to a chunky paste.

2 Transfer to a bowl and stir in the cheese, parsley and some salt and pepper. Spoon into a serving dish and sprinkle a little paprika on top, if you like.

Chicken Liver and Brandy Pâté

This pâté really could not be simpler to make, and tastes so much better than anything you can buy ready-made in the supermarkets. Serve with crispy Melba toast for an elegant appetizer.

SERVES FOUR

1 Heat the butter in a large frying pan until foamy. Add the chicken livers and cook over a medium heat for 3–4 minutes, or until browned and cooked through.

2 Add the brandy and allow to bubble for a few minutes. Let the mixture cool slightly, then tip into a food processor with the cream and some salt and pepper.

3 Process the mixture until smooth and spoon into ramekin dishes. Level the surface and chill overnight to set. Serve garnished with sprigs of parsley to add a little colour.

350g/12oz chicken livers, trimmed and roughly chopped

30ml/2 tbsp brandy

30ml/2 tbsp double (heavy) cream

FROM THE STORECUPBOARD

50g/2oz/¼ cup butter

salt and ground black pepper

Potted Shrimps
with Cayenne Pepper

Cayenne pepper adds a hint of spiciness to this traditional English seaside favourite. Serve with crusty bread or brown toast. The potted shrimps can be stored in the refrigerator for up to 3 days.

SERVES SIX

2 blades of mace

a pinch of cayenne pepper

600ml/1 pint/2½ cups peeled brown shrimps

FROM THE STORECUPBOARD

115g/4oz/½ cup butter, plus extra for greasing

90ml/6 tbsp clarified butter

1 Put the butter, mace and cayenne pepper into a small pan and warm over a gentle heat until melted.

2 Add the peeled shrimps and stir gently until warmed through. Butter six small ramekin dishes.

3 Remove the mace from the shrimp mixture and divide the shrimps and butter evenly between the six ramekins, patting down gently with the back of a spoon. Chill until set.

4 When the butter in the shrimp mixture has set, put the clarified butter in a small pan and melt over a gentle heat. Pour a layer of clarified butter over the top of each ramekin to cover the shrimps and chill again to set.

Marinated Feta
with Lemon and Oregano

The longer the cheese is left to marinate, the better the flavour will be. Serve with tomato and red onion salad and some crisp flatbreads.

SERVES FOUR

200g/7oz Greek feta cheese

1 lemon, cut into wedges

a small handful of fresh oregano sprigs

FROM THE STORECUPBOARD

300ml/½ pint/1¼ cups extra virgin olive oil

1 Drain the feta and pat dry with kitchen paper. Cut it into cubes and arrange in a non-metallic bowl or dish with the lemon wedges and oregano sprigs.

2 Pour the olive oil over the top and cover with clear film (plastic wrap). Chill for at least 3 hours, then serve with a selection of flat breads and salads.

COOK'S TIP *Feta cheese is a salty, crumbly Greek cheese that is usually bought packed in brine. Use a good quality brand and drain thoroughly before using.*

Marinated Anchovies

These tiny fish tend to lose their freshness very quickly so marinating them in garlic and lemon juice is the perfect way to enjoy them. It is probably the simplest way of preparing these fish, because it requires no cooking. Serve them scattered with parsley for a decorative finish.

SERVES FOUR

225g/8oz fresh anchovies, heads and tails removed, and split open along the belly

juice of 3 lemons

2 garlic cloves, finely chopped

FROM THE STORECUPBOARD

30ml/2 tbsp extra virgin olive oil

flaked sea salt

1 Turn the anchovies on to their bellies, and press down along their spine with your thumb. Using the tip of a small knife, carefully remove the backbones from the fish, and arrange the anchovies skin side down in a single layer on a large plate.

2 Squeeze two-thirds of the lemon juice over the fish and sprinkle them with the salt. Cover and leave to stand for 1–24 hours, basting occasionally with the juices, until the flesh is white and no longer translucent.

3 Transfer the anchovies to a serving plate and drizzle with the olive oil and the remaining lemon juice. Scatter the fish with the chopped garlic, then cover with clear film (plastic wrap) and chill until ready to serve.

Chilli Prawn Skewers

Try to get the freshest prawns you can for this recipe. If you buy whole prawns, you will need to remove the heads and shells, leaving the tail section intact. Serve with extra lime wedges.

SERVES FOUR

1 Place eight bamboo skewers in cold water and leave to soak for at least 10 minutes, then preheat the grill (broiler) to high.

2 Thread a prawn on to each skewer, then a lime wedge, then another prawn. Brush the sweet chilli sauce over the prawns and lime wedges.

3 Arrange the skewers on a baking sheet and grill (broil) for about 2 minutes, turning them once, until cooked through. Serve immediately with more chilli sauce for dipping.

16 giant raw prawns (shrimp), shelled with the tail section left intact

1 lime, cut into 8 wedges

60ml/4 tbsp sweet chilli sauce

Crab and Water Chestnut Wontons

Serve these mouthwatering parcels as part of a dim sum selection or with a bowl of soy sauce for dipping as a first course for a Chinese meal. They are also perfect for serving as snacks with drinks at parties as they can be prepared in advance, then steamed at the last minute. Wonton wrappers are available in most Asian food stores and need to be soaked in cold water for a few minutes before use.

SERVES FOUR

1 Finely chop the water chestnuts, mix them with the crab meat and season with salt and pepper.

2 Place about a teaspoonful of the mixture along the centre of each wonton wrapper. Roll up the wontons, tucking in the sides as you go to form a neat parcel.

3 Fill the bottom part of a steamer with boiling water and place the wontons, seam down, in the steamer basket. Sit the basket on top of the water and cover with a tight-fitting lid. Steam for 5–8 minutes, or until the wonton wrappers are tender. Serve hot or warm.

50g/2oz/¹/₃ cup drained, canned water chestnuts

115g/4oz/generous ¹/₂ cup fresh or canned white crab meat

12 wonton wrappers

FROM THE STORECUPBOARD

salt and ground black pepper

Chilli-spiced Chicken Wings

These crispy chicken wings are always the perfect snack for parties and go incredibly well with cold beer! If you like your food spicy, use red hot cayenne pepper in place of the chilli powder. To make a milder version that will be a hit with kids, use sweet paprika in place of the chilli powder. Serve with a fresh tomato and onion salsa for dipping.

SERVES FOUR

12 chicken wings

30ml/2 tbsp plain (all-purpose) flour

15ml/1 tbsp chilli powder

FROM THE STORECUPBOARD

a pinch of salt

sunflower oil, for deep-frying

1 Pat the chicken wings dry with kitchen paper. Mix the flour, chilli powder and salt together and put into a large plastic bag. Add the chicken wings, seal the bag and shake well to coat the chicken wings in the seasoned flour.

2 Heat enough sunflower oil for deep-frying in a large pan and add the chicken wings, three or four at a time. Fry for 8–10 minutes, or until golden and cooked through.

3 Remove the chicken wings with a slotted spoon and drain on kitchen paper. Keep warm in a low oven. Repeat with the remaining chicken wings and serve hot.

Vietnamese Spring Rolls with Pork

You will often find these little spring rolls on the menu in Vietnamese restaurants, called "rice paper rolls". Serve with a chilli dipping sauce.

SERVES FOUR

1 Heat the oil in a frying pan and add the pork. Fry for 5–6 minutes, or until browned. Season well with salt and pepper, stir in the oyster sauce and remove from the heat. Leave to cool.

2 Lay the rice paper wrappers on a clean work surface. Place one-eighth of the pork mixture down one edge of each wrapper. Roll up the wrappers, tucking in the ends as you go to form a roll, and then serve immediately.

350g/12oz/1½ cups minced (ground) pork

30ml/2 tbsp oyster sauce

8 rice-paper roll wrappers

FROM THE STORECUPBOARD

15ml/1 tbsp sunflower oil

salt and ground black pepper

Curried Lamb Samosas

Filo pastry is perfect for making samosas. Once you've mastered folding them, you'll be amazed how quick they are to make.

MAKES TWELVE SAMOSAS

225g/8oz/1 cup minced (ground) lamb

30ml/2 tbsp mild curry paste

12 filo pastry sheets

FROM THE STORECUPBOARD

25g/1oz/2 tbsp butter

salt and ground black pepper

1 Heat a little of the butter in a large pan and add the lamb. Fry for 5–6 minutes, stirring occasionally until browned. Stir in the curry paste and cook for 1–2 minutes. Season and set aside. Preheat the oven to 190°C/375°F/Gas 5.

2 Melt the remaining butter in a pan. Cut the pastry sheets in half lengthways. Brush one strip of pastry with butter, then lay another strip on top and brush with more butter.

3 Place a spoonful of lamb in the corner of the strip and fold over to form a triangle at one end. Keep folding over in the same way to form a triangular package. Brush with butter and place on a baking sheet. Repeat using the remaining pastry. Bake for 15–20 minutes until golden. Serve hot.

Midday Meals

WHAT COULD BE BETTER THAN A TASTY MEAL IN THE
MIDDLE OF THE DAY THAT HAS TAKEN ONLY MOMENTS
TO PREPARE AND NEEDS JUST THREE INGREDIENTS?
WHATEVER YOU'RE IN THE MOOD FOR, WHETHER IT'S
A WARMING BOWL OF SOUP, A HEALTHY SALAD, A
GOURMET SANDWICH OR A BOWL OF PASTA – THERE'S
SOMETHING HERE FOR EVERYONE. THE RECIPES ARE
ALL SO SIMPLE THAT YOU CAN EASILY REDUCE OR
INCREASE THE PROPORTIONS TO MAKE A QUICK LUNCH
FOR ONE, OR A HEALTHY MEAL FOR THE WHOLE FAMILY.

Curried Cauliflower Soup

This spicy, creamy soup is perfect for lunch on a cold winter's day served with crusty bread and garnished with fresh coriander (cilantro). You can also make broccoli soup in the same way, using the same weight of broccoli in place of the cauliflower.

SERVES FOUR

750ml/1¼ pints/3 cups milk

1 large cauliflower

15ml/1 tbsp garam masala

FROM THE STORECUPBOARD

salt and ground black pepper

1 Pour the milk into a large pan and place over a medium heat. Cut the cauliflower into florets and add to the milk with the garam masala and season with salt and pepper.

2 Bring the milk to the boil, then reduce the heat, partially cover the pan with a lid and simmer for about 20 minutes, or until the cauliflower is tender.

3 Let the mixture cool for a few minutes, then transfer to a food processor and process until smooth (you may have to do this in two batches). Return the purée to the pan and heat through gently, checking and adjusting the seasoning, and serve immediately.

Tuscan Bean Soup

Cavolo nero is a very dark green cabbage with a nutty flavour from Tuscany and southern Italy. It is ideal for this traditional recipe. It is available in most large supermarkets, but if you can't get it, use Savoy cabbage instead. Serve with ciabatta bread.

SERVES FOUR

2 x 400g/14oz cans chopped tomatoes with herbs

250g/9oz cavolo nero leaves

400g/14oz can cannellini beans

FROM THE STORECUPBOARD

60ml/4 tbsp extra virgin olive oil

salt and ground black pepper

1 Pour the tomatoes into a large pan and add a can of cold water. Season with salt and pepper and bring to the boil, then reduce the heat to a simmer.

2 Roughly shred the cabbage leaves and add them to the pan. Partially cover the pan and simmer gently for about 15 minutes, or until the cabbage is tender.

3 Drain and rinse the cannellini beans, add to the pan and warm through for a few minutes. Check and adjust the seasoning, then ladle the soup into bowls and drizzle each one with a little olive oil and serve.

Pea Soup with Garlic

If you keep peas in the freezer, you can rustle up this delicious soup in minutes. It has a wonderfully sweet taste and smooth texture and is great served with crusty bread and garnished with mint.

SERVES FOUR

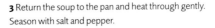

1 Heat the butter in a large pan and add the garlic. Fry gently for 2–3 minutes, until softened, then add the peas. Cook for 1–2 minutes more, then pour in the stock.

2 Bring the soup to the boil, then reduce the heat to a simmer. Cover the pan and cook for 5–6 minutes, until the peas are tender. Leave to cool slightly, then transfer the mixture to a food processor and process or until smooth (you may have to do this in two batches).

3 Return the soup to the pan and heat through gently. Season with salt and pepper.

1 garlic clove, crushed

900g/2lb/8 cups frozen peas

1.2 litres/2 pints/5 cups chicken stock

FROM THE STORECUPBOARD

25g/1oz/2 tbsp butter

salt and ground black pepper

Pea and Mint Omelette

Serve this deliciously light omelette with crusty bread and a green salad for a fresh and tasty lunch. If you're making the omelette for a summer lunch when peas are in season, use freshly shelled peas instead of frozen ones.

SERVES TWO

1 Cook the peas in a large pan of salted boiling water for 3–4 minutes until tender. Drain well and set aside. Break the eggs into a large bowl and beat with a fork. Season well with salt and pepper, then stir in the peas and chopped mint.

2 Heat the butter in a medium frying pan until foamy. Pour in the egg mixture and cook over a medium heat for 3–4 minutes, drawing in the cooked egg from the edges from time to time, until the mixture is nearly set.

3 Finish off cooking the omelette under a hot grill (broiler) until set and golden. Carefully fold the omelette over, cut it in half and serve immediately.

50g/2oz/¹/₂ cup frozen peas

4 eggs

30ml/2 tbsp chopped fresh mint

FROM THE STORECUPBOARD

a knob (pat) of butter

salt and ground black pepper

Seared Tuna Niçoise

A traditional tuna Niçoise consists of tuna, olives, green beans, potatoes and eggs, but this modern version using fresh tuna is a simplified one – although just as tasty. Serve it with a green salad.

SERVES FOUR

1 Put the tuna steaks in a shallow non-metallic dish. Mix the oil and vinegar together and season with salt and pepper.

2 Pour the mixture over the tuna steaks and turn them to coat in the marinade. Cover and chill for up to 1 hour.

3 Heat a griddle pan until smoking hot. Remove the tuna steaks from the marinade and lay them on the griddle pan. Cook for 2–3 minutes on each side, so that they are still pink in the centre. Remove from the pan and set aside.

4 Meanwhile, cook the eggs in a pan of boiling water for 5–6 minutes, then cool under cold running water. Shell the eggs and cut in half lengthways.

5 Pour the marinade on to the griddle pan and cook until it starts to bubble. Divide the tuna steaks among four serving plates and top each with half an egg. Drizzle the marinade over the top and serve immediately.

4 tuna steaks, about 150g/5oz each

30ml/2 tbsp sherry vinegar

2 eggs

FROM THE STORECUPBOARD

45ml/3 tbsp garlic-infused olive oil

salt and ground black pepper

Creamy Parmesan-Baked Eggs

These eggs are delicious as they are but can easily be "dressed up" with additional ingredients. Try adding chopped smoked ham and parsley before you cook them. Serve with thinly sliced bread and butter.

SERVES TWO

1 Preheat the oven to 160°C/325°F/Gas 3. Break the eggs into four ramekin dishes and spoon the cream over the top. Season with salt and ground black pepper and sprinkle the Parmesan cheese on top.

2 Bake the eggs for about 10 minutes, or until they are just set, and serve immediately.

COOK'S TIPS
• Serve these rich and creamy eggs with a leafy green salad flavoured with fresh tarragon.
• For the best results, be sure to serve the eggs as soon as they are cooked.

4 large (US extra large) eggs

60ml/4 tbsp double (heavy) cream

30ml/2 tbsp freshly grated Parmesan cheese

FROM THE STORECUPBOARD

salt and ground black pepper

Grilled Aubergine, Mint and Couscous Salad

Packets of flavoured couscous are available in most supermarkets – you can use whichever you like, but garlic and coriander is particularly good for this recipe. Serve with a crisp green salad.

SERVES TWO

1 large aubergine (eggplant)

115g/4oz packet garlic-and-coriander (cilantro) flavoured couscous

30ml/2 tbsp chopped fresh mint

FROM THE STORECUPBOARD

30ml/2 tbsp olive oil

salt and ground black pepper

1 Preheat the grill (broiler) to high. Cut the aubergine into large chunky pieces and toss them with the olive oil. Season with salt and pepper to taste and spread the aubergine pieces on a non-stick baking sheet. Grill for 5–6 minutes, turning occasionally, until golden brown.

2 Meanwhile, prepare the couscous according to the instructions on the packet. Stir the grilled aubergine and chopped mint into the couscous, toss thoroughly and serve immediately.

Marinated Courgette and Flageolet Bean Salad

Serve this healthy salad as a light lunch or as an accompaniment to meat and chicken dishes. It has a wonderful bright green colour and is perfect for a summer lunch.

SERVES FOUR

2 courgettes (zucchini), halved lengthways and sliced

400g/14oz can flageolet beans, drained and rinsed

grated rind and juice of 1 unwaxed lemon

FROM THE STORECUPBOARD

45ml/3 tbsp garlic-infused olive oil

salt and ground black pepper

1 Cook the courgettes in boiling salted water for 2–3 minutes, or until just tender. Drain well and refresh under cold running water.

2 Transfer the drained courgettes into a bowl with the beans and stir in the oil, lemon rind and juice and some salt and pepper. Chill for 30 minutes before serving.

VARIATION *To add extra flavour to the salad add 30ml/2 tbsp chopped fresh herbs before chilling. Basil and mint both have fresh, distinctive flavours that will work very well.*

Roasted Pepper and Hummus Wrap

Wraps make a tasty change to sandwiches and have the bonus that they can be made a few hours in advance without going soggy in the way that bread sandwiches often can. You can introduce all kinds of variation to this basic combination. Try using roasted aubergine (eggplant) in place of the red peppers, or guacamole in place of the hummus. As well as plain flour tortillas, you can also buy flavoured tortillas from most supermarkets.

SERVES TWO

1 large red (bell) pepper, halved and seeded

4 tbsp hummus

2 soft flour tortillas

FROM THE STORECUPBOARD

15ml/1 tbsp olive oil

salt and ground black pepper

1 Preheat the grill (broiler) to high. Brush the pepper halves with the oil and place cut side down on a baking sheet. Grill for 5 minutes, until charred. Put the pepper halves in a sealed plastic bag and leave to cool.

2 When cooled, remove the peppers from the bag and carefully peel away the charred skin and discard. Thinly slice the flesh using a sharp knife.

3 Spread the hummus over the tortillas in a thin, even layer and top with the roasted pepper slices. Season with salt and plenty of ground black pepper, then roll them up and cut in half to serve.

Focaccia with Sardines and Roast Tomatoes

Fresh sardines not only have a lovely flavour and texture, but they are also cheap to buy – so make an economical yet utterly delicious lunch.

SERVES FOUR

20 cherry tomatoes

12 fresh sardine fillets

1 focaccia loaf

FROM THE STORECUPBOARD

45ml/3 tbsp herb-infused olive oil

salt and ground black pepper

1 Preheat the oven to 190°C/375°F/Gas 5. Put the cherry tomatoes in a small roasting pan and drizzle 30ml/2 tbsp of the oil over the top. Season with salt and pepper and roast for 10–15 minutes, or until tender and slightly charred. Remove from the oven and set aside.

2 Preheat the grill (broiler) to high. Brush the sardine fillets with the remaining oil and lay them on a baking sheet. Grill for 4–5 minutes on each side, until cooked through.

3 Split the focaccia in half horizontally and cut each piece in half to give four equal pieces. Toast the cut side under the grill until golden. Top with the sardines and tomatoes and an extra drizzle of oil. Season with black pepper then serve.

Toasted Sourdough with Goat's Cheese

Choose a good quality, firm goat's cheese for this recipe because it needs to keep its shape during cooking. Serve with fresh rocket leaves.

SERVES TWO

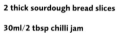

2 thick sourdough bread slices

30ml/2 tbsp chilli jam

2 firm goat's cheese slices, about 90g/3½oz each

FROM THE STORECUPBOARD

30ml/2 tbsp garlic-infused olive oil

ground black pepper

1 Preheat the grill (broiler) to high. Brush the sourdough bread on both sides with the oil, and grill (broil) one side until golden. Spread the un-toasted side of each slice with the chilli jam and top with the goat's cheese.

2 Return the bread to the grill and cook for 3–4 minutes, or until the cheese is beginning to melt and turn golden and bubbling. Season with ground black pepper and serve immediately with rocket (arugula) leaves.

Steak and Blue Cheese Sandwiches

Many people like their rib eye steaks cooked quite rare in the centre, but how you like yours is up to you. Add a couple of minutes to the cooking time if you prefer them more well done.

SERVES TWO

1 Bake the ciabatta according to the instructions on the packet. Remove from the oven and leave to rest for a few minutes. Cut the loaf in half and split each half horizontally.

2 Heat a griddle pan until hot. Brush the steaks with the olive oil and lay them on the griddle pan. Cook for 2–3 minutes on each side, depending on the thickness of the steaks.

3 Remove the steaks from the pan and set aside to rest for a few minutes. Cut them in half and place in the sandwiches with the cheese. Season with salt and pepper, and serve.

1 ready-to-bake ciabatta bread

2 rib eye steaks, about 200g/7oz each

115g/4oz Gorgonzola cheese, sliced

FROM THE STORECUPBOARD

15ml/1 tbsp olive oil

salt and ground black pepper

Warm Penne with Fresh Tomatoes and Basil

This dish is fresh, healthy and ready in minutes. It is the perfect way to use up a glut of ripe summer tomatoes.

SERVES FOUR

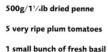

500g/1¼lb dried penne

5 very ripe plum tomatoes

1 small bunch of fresh basil

FROM THE STORECUPBOARD

60ml/4 tbsp extra virgin olive oil

salt and ground black pepper

1 Cook the pasta in plenty of salted, boiling water according to the instructions on the packet. Meanwhile, roughly chop the tomatoes, pull the basil leaves from their stems and tear up the leaves.

2 Drain the pasta thoroughly and toss with the tomatoes, basil and olive oil. Season with salt and freshly ground black pepper and serve immediately.

COOK'S TIP *If you cannot find ripe tomatoes, roast them to bring out their flavour. Put the tomatoes in a roasting pan, drizzle with oil and roast at 190°C/375°F/ Gas 5 for 20 minutes, then mash roughly.*

Broccoli and Chilli Spaghetti

The contrast between the hot chilli and the mild broccoli is delicious and goes perfectly with spaghetti. To add extra flavour and texture, sprinkle the spaghetti and broccoli with toasted pine nuts and grated or shaved Parmesan cheese just before serving.

SERVES FOUR

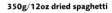

350g/12oz dried spaghetti

450g/1lb broccoli, cut into small florets

1 fat red chilli, seeded and finely chopped

FROM THE STORECUPBOARD

150ml/¼ pint/⅔ cup garlic-infused olive oil

salt and ground black pepper

1 Bring a large pan of lightly salted water to the boil. Add the spaghetti and broccoli and cook for 8–10 minutes, until both are tender. Drain thoroughly.

2 Using the back of a fork crush the broccoli roughly, taking care not to mash the spaghetti strands at the same time.

3 Meanwhile, warm the oil and finely chopped chilli in a small pan over a low heat and cook very gently for 5 minutes.

4 Pour the chilli and oil over the spaghetti and broccoli and toss together to combine. Season to taste. Divide between four warmed bowls and serve immediately.

Spicy Chorizo Sausage and Spring Onion Hash

Use up leftover boiled potatoes for this recipe. Fresh chorizo sausages are available from good butchers and Spanish delis.

SERVES FOUR

1 Heat a large frying pan over a medium heat and add the sausages. Cook for 8–10 minutes, turning occasionally, until cooked through. Remove from the pan and set aside.

2 Add the olive oil to the sausage fat in the pan and then add the potatoes. Cook over a low heat for 5–8 minutes, turning occasionally until golden. Meanwhile, cut the sausages into bite-size chunks and add to the pan.

3 Add the spring onions to the pan and cook for a couple more minutes, until they are piping hot. Season with salt and pepper, and serve immediately.

450g/1lb fresh chorizo sausages

450g/1lb cooked potatoes, diced

1 bunch of spring onions (scallions), sliced

FROM THE STORECUPBOARD

15ml/1 tbsp olive oil

salt and ground black pepper

Baked Sweet Potatoes with Leeks and Gorgonzola

This dish tastes wonderful and looks stunning if you buy the beautiful orange-fleshed sweet potatoes.

SERVES FOUR

4 large sweet potatoes, scrubbed

2 large leeks, washed and sliced

115g/4oz Gorgonzola cheese, sliced

FROM THE STORECUPBOARD

30ml/2 tbsp olive oil

salt and ground black pepper

1 Preheat the oven to 190°C/375°F/Gas 5. Dry the sweet potatoes with kitchen paper and rub them all over with 15ml/ 1 tbsp of the oil. Place them on a baking sheet and sprinkle with salt. Bake for 1 hour, or until tender.

2 Meanwhile, heat the remaining oil in a frying pan and add the sliced leeks. Cook for 3–4 minutes, or until softened and just beginning to turn golden.

3 Cut the potatoes in half lengthways and place them cut side up on the baking sheet. Top with the cooked leeks and season.

4 Lay the cheese slices on top and grill (broil) under a hot grill for 2–3 minutes, until the cheese is bubbling. Serve immediately.

Simple Suppers

AFTER A LONG, HARD DAY, THERE'S NOTHING BETTER
THAN COMING HOME TO A DELICIOUS, WARMING
EVENING MEAL. THIS CHAPTER IS FULL OF TEMPTING
IDEAS THAT ARE QUICK AND SIMPLE TO MAKE AND
OFFER ALL THE COMFORT OF A SUPPER THAT HAS
TAKEN HOURS TO PREPARE. TRY GRILLED HAKE WITH
LEMON AND CHILLI, BAKED HONEY MUSTARD CHICKEN,
SIMPLE POTATO GNOCCHI OR MINTY COURGETTE
LINGUINE. EACH DISH IS EASY AND FLAVOURSOME AND
YOU'LL FIND IT EASY TO SIT BACK, RELAX AND UNWIND.

Minty Courgette Linguine

Sweet, mild courgettes and refreshing mint are a great combination and are delicious with pasta. Dried linguine has been used here but you can use any type of pasta you like. Couscous also works well in place of pasta if you prefer.

SERVES FOUR

450g/1lb dried linguine

4 small courgettes (zucchini), sliced

1 small bunch of fresh mint, roughly chopped

FROM THE STORECUPBOARD

75ml/5 tbsp garlic-infused olive oil

salt and ground black pepper

1 Cook the linguine in plenty of salted, boiling water according to the instructions on the packet.

2 Meanwhile, heat 45ml/3 tbsp of the oil in a large frying pan and add the courgettes. Fry for 2–3 minutes, stirring occasionally, until they are tender and golden.

3 Drain the pasta well and toss with the courgettes and chopped mint. Season with salt and pepper, drizzle over the remaining oil and serve immediately.

Pasta with Roast Tomatoes and Goat's Cheese

Roasting tomatoes brings out their flavour and sweetness, which contrasts perfectly with the sharp taste and creamy texture of goat's cheese. Serve with a crisp green salad flavoured with herbs.

SERVES FOUR

8 large ripe tomatoes

450g/1lb any dried pasta shapes

200g/7oz firm goat's cheese, crumbled

FROM THE STORECUPBOARD

60ml/4 tbsp garlic-infused olive oil

salt and ground black pepper

1 Preheat the oven to 190°C/375°F/Gas 5. Place the tomatoes in a roasting pan and drizzle over 30ml/2 tbsp of the oil. Season well with salt and pepper and roast for 20–25 minutes, or until soft and slightly charred.

2 Meanwhile, cook the pasta in plenty of salted, boiling water, according to the instructions on the packet. Drain well and return to the pan.

3 Roughly mash the tomatoes with a fork, and stir the contents of the roasting pan into the pasta. Gently stir in the goat's cheese and the remaining oil and serve.

Linguine with Anchovies and Capers

This is a fantastic storecupboard recipe. Use salted capers if you can find them, as they have a better flavour than the bottled ones, but remember that you need to rinse them thoroughly before using. Be sure to chop the anchovies finely so that they "melt" into the sauce.

SERVES FOUR

450g/1lb dried linguine

8 anchovy fillets, drained

30ml/2 tbsp salted capers, thoroughly rinsed and drained

FROM THE STORECUPBOARD

75ml/5 tbsp garlic-infused olive oil

salt and ground black pepper

1 Cook the linguine in plenty of salted, boiling water according to the instructions on the packet.

2 Meanwhile, finely chop the anchovy fillets and place in a small pan with the oil and some black pepper. Heat very gently for 5 minutes, stirring occasionally, until the anchovies start to disintegrate.

3 Drain the pasta thoroughly and toss with the anchovies, oil and capers. Season with a little salt and plenty of black pepper to taste. Divide between warmed bowls and serve immediately.

Home-made Potato Gnocchi

These classic Italian potato dumplings are very simple to make – it just requires a little patience when it comes to shaping them. Serve them as soon as they are cooked, tossed in melted butter and fresh sage leaves, sprinkled with grated Parmesan cheese and plenty of black pepper. They make a fabulous alternative to pasta.

900g/2lb floury potatoes, cut into large chunks

2 eggs, beaten

150–175g/5–6oz/1¹/₄–1¹/₂ cups plain (all-purpose) flour

FROM THE STORECUPBOARD

10ml/2 tsp salt

SERVES TWO

1 Cook the potatoes in salted, boiling water for 15 minutes, until tender. Drain well and return to the pan, set it over a low heat and dry the potatoes for 1–2 minutes.

2 Mash the potatoes until smooth, then gradually stir in the eggs and salt. Work in enough flour to form a soft dough.

3 Break off small pieces of the dough and roll into balls, using floured hands. Press the back of a fork into each ball to make indentations. Repeat until all the dough has been used. Leave the gnocchi to rest for 15–20 minutes before cooking.

4 Bring a large pan of water to a gentle boil. Add the gnocchi, about ten at a time, and cook for 3–4 minutes, or until they float to the surface. Drain thoroughly and serve as soon as all the gnocchi have been cooked.

VARIATION To make herb-flavoured gnocchi, add 45ml/3 tbsp chopped fresh herbs, such as basil, parsley and sage, to the potato and flour dough and combine well. Serve with butter and grated Parmesan.

Classic Margherita Pizza

Bought pizza base mixes are a great storecupboard stand-by. A Margherita Pizza makes a lovely simple supper, but of course you can add any extra toppings you like. Prosciutto and rocket (arugula) make a great addition – just add them to the pizza after it is cooked.

SERVES TWO

half a 300g/11oz packet pizza base mix

45ml/3 tbsp ready-made tomato and basil sauce

150g/5oz mozzarella, sliced

FROM THE STORECUPBOARD

15ml/1 tbsp herb-infused olive oil

salt and ground black pepper

1 Make the pizza base mix according to the instructions on the packet. Brush the base with a little of the olive oil and spread over the tomato and basil sauce, not quite to the edges.

2 Arrange the slices of mozzarella on top of the pizza and bake for 25–30 minutes, or until golden.

3 Drizzle the remaining oil on top of the pizza, season with salt and black pepper and serve immediately, garnished with fresh basil leaves.

Cheesy Leek and Couscous Cake

The tangy flavour of sharp Cheddar cheese goes perfectly with the sweet taste of leeks. The cheese melts into the couscous and helps it stick together, making a firm cake that's easy to cut into wedges. Serve with a crisp green salad.

SERVES FOUR

300g/11oz couscous

2 leeks, sliced

200g/7oz mature Cheddar or Monterey Jack, grated

FROM THE STORECUPBOARD

45ml/3 tbsp olive oil

salt and ground black pepper

VARIATION *There are endless variations on this tangy, tasty cake but choose a cheese that melts well because it will help the cake to stick together. Try using caramelized onions and blue cheese in place of the leeks and Cheddar.*

1 Put the couscous in a large heatproof bowl and pour over 450ml/³⁄₄ pint/scant 2 cups boiling water. Cover and set aside for about 15 minutes, or until all the water has been absorbed.

2 Heat 15ml/1 tbsp of the oil in a 23cm/9in non-stick frying pan. Add the leeks and cook over a medium heat for 4–5 minutes, stirring occasionally, until tender and golden.

3 Remove the leeks with a slotted spoon and stir them into the couscous. Add the grated cheese and some salt and pepper and stir through. Heat the remaining oil in the pan and tip in the couscous and leek mixture. Pat down firmly to form a cake and cook over a fairly gentle heat for 15 minutes, or until the underside is crisp and golden.

4 Slide the couscous cake onto a plate, then invert it back into the pan to cook the other side. Cook for a further 5–8 minutes, or until golden, then remove from the heat. Slide on to a board and serve cut into wedges.

Salt Cod and Potato Fritters

These little fritters are extremely easy to make and taste delicious. Serve them simply with a wedge of fresh lemon and some watercress or green salad. Offer a bowl of garlic mayonnaise for dipping.

MAKES ABOUT TWENTY FOUR

450g/1lb salt cod fillets

500g/1¼lb floury potatoes, unpeeled

plain (all-purpose) flour, for coating

FROM THE STORECUPBOARD

vegetable oil, for deep-frying

salt and ground black pepper

1 Put the salt cod in a bowl, pour over cold water and leave to soak for 24 hours, changing the water every 6–8 hours. Drain, rinse and place in a pan of cold water. Slowly bring to the boil and simmer for 5 minutes, then drain and cool. When cooled, remove any bones and skin and mash the fish with a fork.

2 Cook the potatoes in their skins in a pan of salted boiling water for 20–25 minutes, or until just tender. Peel and mash.

3 Add the fish to the potatoes and mix well. Season to taste with salt and pepper. Break off walnut-sized pieces of the mixture and roll into balls. Place on a floured plate, cover and chill for 20–30 minutes. Roll each ball lightly in flour, dusting off any excess.

4 Heat enough oil for deep-frying in a large pan and fry the balls for 5–6 minutes, or until golden. Remove with a slotted spoon and drain on kitchen paper. Serve hot or warm.

Asian-style Crab Cakes

You could serve these patties as a simple supper, or an appetizer for eight people. Use a mixture of white and brown crab meat, as the dark adds a depth of flavour and texture. Serve with sweet chilli sauce.

MAKES SIXTEEN

450g/1lb/2²/₃ cups fresh crab meat, white and brown

15ml/1 tbsp grated fresh root ginger

15–30ml/1–2 tbsp plain (all-purpose) flour

FROM THE STORECUPBOARD

60ml/4 tbsp sunflower oil

salt and ground black pepper

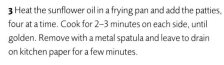

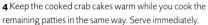

1 Put the crab meat in a bowl and add the ginger, some salt and ground black pepper and the flour. Stir well until thoroughly mixed.

2 Using floured hands, divide the mixture into 16 equal-sized pieces and shape roughly into patties.

3 Heat the sunflower oil in a frying pan and add the patties, four at a time. Cook for 2–3 minutes on each side, until golden. Remove with a metal spatula and leave to drain on kitchen paper for a few minutes.

4 Keep the cooked crab cakes warm while you cook the remaining patties in the same way. Serve immediately.

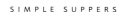

Grilled Hake with Lemon and Chilli

Choose firm hake fillets, as thick as possible. This is an ideal recipe if you are counting the calories, because it is low in fat. Serve with new potatoes and steamed fine green beans. Or, if you're not counting calories, serve with creamy mashed potatoes with plenty of butter stirred in.

SERVES FOUR

4 hake fillets, each 150g/5oz

finely grated rind and juice of 1 unwaxed lemon

15ml/1 tbsp crushed chilli flakes

FROM THE STORECUPBOARD

30ml/2 tbsp olive oil

salt and ground black pepper

1 Preheat the grill (broiler) to high. Brush the hake fillets all over with the olive oil and place them skin side up on a baking sheet.

2 Grill (broil) the fish for 4–5 minutes, until the skin is crispy, then carefully turn them over using a metal spatula.

3 Sprinkle the fillets with the lemon rind and chilli flakes and season with salt and ground black pepper.

4 Grill the fillets for a further 2–3 minutes, or until the hake is cooked through. (Test using the point of a sharp knife; the flesh should flake.) Squeeze over the lemon juice just before serving.

Honey Mustard Chicken

Chicken thighs have a rich flavour, but if you want to cut down on fat, use four chicken breast portions instead and cook for 20–25 minutes. Serve with a chunky tomato and red onion salad.

SERVES FOUR

1 Preheat the oven to 190°C/375°F/Gas 5. Put the chicken thighs in a single layer in a roasting pan.

2 Mix together the mustard and honey, season with salt and ground black pepper to taste and brush the mixture all over the chicken thighs.

3 Cook for 25–30 minutes, brushing the chicken with the pan juices occasionally, until cooked through. (To check the chicken is cooked through, skewer it with a sharp knife; the juices should run clear.)

8 chicken thighs

60ml/4 tbsp wholegrain mustard

60ml/4 tbsp clear honey

FROM THE STORECUPBOARD

salt and ground black pepper

Stir-fried Chicken with Thai Basil

Thai basil, sometimes called holy basil, has purple-tinged leaves and a more pronounced, slightly aniseedy flavour than the usual varieties. It is available in most Asian food stores but if you can't find any, use a handful of ordinary basil instead. Serve this fragrant stir-fry with plain steamed rice or boiled noodles and soy sauce on the side.

SERVES FOUR

1 Using a sharp knife, slice the chicken breast portions into strips. Halve the peppers, remove the seeds, then cut each piece of pepper into strips.

2 Heat the oil in a wok or large frying pan. Add the chicken and red peppers and stir-fry over a high heat for about 3 minutes, until the chicken is golden and cooked through. Season with salt and ground black pepper.

3 Roughly tear up the basil leaves, add to the chicken and peppers and toss briefly to combine. Serve immediately.

4 skinless chicken breast fillets, cut into strips

2 red (bell) peppers

1 small bunch of fresh Thai basil

FROM THE STORECUPBOARD

30ml/2 tbsp garlic-infused olive oil

salt and ground black pepper

Crème Fraîche and Coriander Chicken

Boneless chicken thighs are used for this recipe but you can substitute breast portions if you like. Be generous with the coriander leaves, as they have a wonderful fragrant flavour, or use chopped parsley instead. Serve with creamy mashed potatoes. To make a lower fat version of this dish, use chicken breast portions and low-fat crème fraîche.

SERVES FOUR

6 skinless chicken thigh fillets

60ml/4 tbsp crème fraîche

1 small bunch of fresh coriander (cilantro), roughly chopped

FROM THE STORECUPBOARD

15ml/1 tbsp sunflower oil

salt and ground black pepper

1 Cut each chicken thigh into three or four pieces. Heat the oil in a large frying pan, add the chicken and cook for about 6 minutes, turning occasionally, until cooked through.

2 Add the crème fraîche to the pan and stir until melted, then allow to bubble for 1–2 minutes.

3 Add the chopped coriander to the chicken and stir to combine. Season with salt and ground black pepper to taste, and serve immediately.

Fragrant Lemon Grass and Ginger Pork Patties

Lemon grass lends a fragrant citrus flavour to pork, enhanced by the fresh zing of ginger. Serve the patties in burger buns with thick slices of juicy tomato, crisp, refreshing lettuce and a splash of chilli sauce.

SERVES FOUR

450g/1lb/2 cups minced (ground) pork

15ml/1 tbsp fresh root ginger, grated

1 lemon grass stalk

FROM THE STORECUPBOARD

30ml/2 tbsp sunflower oil

salt and ground black pepper

1 Put the pork in a bowl and stir in the ginger. Season with salt and pepper. Remove the tough outer layers from the lemon grass stalk and discard. Chop the centre part as finely as possible and mix into the pork. Shape into four patties and chill for about 20 minutes.

2 Heat the oil in a large, non-stick frying pan and add the patties. Fry for 3–4 minutes on each side over a gentle heat, until cooked through. Remove from the pan with a metal spatula and drain on kitchen paper, then serve.

Pan-fried Gammon with Cider

Gammon and cider are a delicious combination with the sweet, tangy flavour of cider complementing the gammon perfectly. Serve with mustard mashed potatoes.

4 gammon steaks (smoked or cured ham), 225g/8oz each

150ml/^{1}/$_4$ pint/^{2}/$_3$ cup dry (hard) cider

45ml/3 tbsp double (heavy) cream

FROM THE STORECUPBOARD

30ml/2 tbsp sunflower oil

salt and ground black pepper

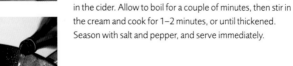

SERVES FOUR

1 Heat the oil in a large frying pan until hot. Neatly snip the rind on the gammon steaks to stop them curling up and add them to the pan.

2 Cook the steaks for 3–4 minutes on each side, then pour in the cider. Allow to boil for a couple of minutes, then stir in the cream and cook for 1–2 minutes, or until thickened. Season with salt and pepper, and serve immediately.

Caramelized Onion and Sausage Tarte Tatin

Toulouse sausages have a garlicky flavour and meaty texture that is delicious with fried onions. Serve with a green salad of bitter leaves.

SERVES FOUR

450g/1lb Toulouse sausages

2 large onions, sliced

250g/9oz ready-made puff pastry, thawed if frozen

FROM THE STORECUPBOARD

45ml/3 tbsp sunflower oil

salt and ground black pepper

1 Heat the oil in a 23cm/9in non-stick frying pan with an ovenproof handle, and add the sausages. Cook over a gentle heat, turning occasionally, for 7–10 minutes, or until golden and cooked through. Remove from the pan and set aside.

2 Preheat the oven to 190°C/375°F/Gas 5. Pour the remaining oil into the frying pan and add the onions. Season with salt and pepper and cook over a gentle heat for 10 minutes, stirring occasionally, until caramelized and tender.

3 Slice each sausage into four or five chunks and stir into the onions. Remove from the heat and set aside.

4 Roll out the puff pastry and cut out a circle slightly larger than the frying pan. Lay the pastry over the sausages and onions, tucking the edges in all the way around. Bake for 20 minutes, or until the pastry is risen and golden. Turn out on to a board, pastry side down, cut into wedges and serve.

Marinated Lamb with Oregano and Basil

Lamb leg steaks are chunky with a sweet flavour and go well with oregano and basil. However, you could also use finely chopped rosemary or thyme. Serve with couscous.

SERVES FOUR

1 Put the lamb in a shallow, non-metallic dish. Mix 45ml/3 tbsp of the oil with the oregano, basil and some salt and pepper, reserving some of the herbs for garnish. Pour over the lamb and turn to coat in the marinade. Cover and chill for up to 8 hours.

2 Heat the remaining oil in a large frying pan. Remove the lamb from the marinade and fry for 5–6 minutes on each side, until slightly pink in the centre. Add the marinade and cook for 1–2 minutes until warmed through. Garnish with the reserved herbs and serve.

4 large or 8 small lamb leg steaks

1 small bunch of fresh oregano, roughly chopped

1 small bunch of fresh basil, torn

FROM THE STORECUPBOARD

60ml/4 tbsp garlic-infused olive oil

salt and ground black pepper

Take Your Time

THIS CHAPTER IS DEVOTED TO THOSE DELICIOUS
DISHES THAT YOU NEED TO PLAN AHEAD FOR. THEY
MAY REQUIRE LENGTHY PREPARATION OR SLOW
COOKING BUT THEY STILL NEED ONLY THREE MAIN
INGREDIENTS. THERE ARE FABULOUS ROASTS AND
OVEN-BAKED DISHES, SENSATIONAL STEWS AND
WONDERFULLY FLAVOURSOME MARINATED DISHES TO
CHOOSE FROM. ENJOY THEM WHEN YOU'VE GOT TIME
ON YOUR HANDS — FOR A SPECIAL DINNER OR FOR A
LEISURELY SUNDAY LUNCH WITH ALL THE FAMILY.

25g/1oz/¹/₂ cup dried porcini mushrooms

1 onion, finely chopped

225g/8oz/generous 1 cup risotto rice

FROM THE STORECUPBOARD

30ml/2 tbsp garlic-infused olive oil

salt and ground black pepper

Oven-baked Porcini Risotto

This risotto is easy to make because you don't have to stand over it stirring constantly as it cooks, as you do with a traditional risotto.

SERVES FOUR

1 Put the mushrooms in a heatproof bowl and pour over 750ml/1¹/₄ pints/3 cups boiling water. Leave to soak for 30 minutes. Drain the mushrooms through a sieve lined with kitchen paper, reserving the soaking liquor. Rinse the mushrooms thoroughly under running water to remove any grit, and dry on kitchen paper.

2 Preheat the oven to 180°C/350°F/Gas 4. Heat the oil in a roasting pan on the hob and add the onion. Cook for 2–3 minutes, or until softened but not coloured.

3 Add the rice and stir for 1–2 minutes, then add the mushrooms and stir. Pour in the mushroom liquor and mix well. Season with salt and pepper, and cover with foil.

4 Bake in the oven for 30 minutes, stirring occasionally, until all the stock has been absorbed and the rice is tender. Divide between warm serving bowls and serve immediately.

Creamy Red Lentil Dhal

This makes a tasty winter supper for vegetarians and meat eaters alike. Serve with naan bread, coconut cream and fresh coriander (cilantro) leaves. The coconut cream gives this dish a really rich taste.

SERVES FOUR

1 Heat the oil in a large pan and add the lentils. Fry for 1–2 minutes, stirring continuously, then stir in the curry paste and 600ml/1 pint/2^1/$_2$ cups boiling water.

2 Bring the mixture to the boil, then reduce the heat to a gentle simmer. Cover the pan and cook for 15 minutes, stirring occasionally, until the lentils are tender and the mixture has thickened.

3 Season the dhal with plenty of salt and ground black pepper to taste, and serve piping hot.

150g/5oz/^{2}/$_3$ cup red lentils

15ml/1 tbsp hot curry paste

FROM THE STORECUPBOARD

15ml/1 tbsp sunflower oil

salt and ground black pepper

Potato, Pancetta and Parmesan Galette

This richly flavoured "pie" is a perfect winter warmer. A mandolin will make quick work of the potatoes – slicing them thinly – but be careful of your fingers because the blade is sharp.

SERVES FOUR

1 Preheat the oven to 180°C/350°F/Gas 4. Brush a 20cm/8in ovenproof dish with some of the oil. Arrange one-third of the potatoes in the bottom of the dish, season and lay three slices of pancetta over the top. Sprinkle over a little cheese and arrange another layer of potatoes on the top.

2 Lay the remaining pancetta on top of the potatoes and sprinkle with a little more Parmesan and seasoning. Top with the remaining potatoes, season with salt and pepper and drizzle over the remaining olive oil. Press the potatoes down firmly and cover the tin with foil.

3 Bake for 30–35 minutes, then uncover and sprinkle with the remaining Parmesan. Bake for a further 15–20 minutes, or until golden. Leave to rest for about 10 minutes, then cut into wedges to serve.

450g/1lb waxy potatoes, peeled and very thinly sliced

6 pancetta slices

50g/2oz/²/₃ cup freshly grated Parmesan cheese

FROM THE STORECUPBOARD

30ml/2 tbsp garlic-infused olive oil

salt and ground black pepper

Roast Acorn Squash with Spinach and Gorgonzola

Roasting squash brings out its sweetness, here offset by tangy cheese. Acorn squash has been used here, but any type of squash will give delicious results.

SERVES FOUR

1 Preheat the oven to 190°C/375°F/Gas 5. Cut the tops off the squash, and scoop out and discard the seeds. Place the squash, cut side up, in a roasting pan and drizzle with 30ml/2 tbsp of the oil. Season with salt and pepper and bake for 30–40 minutes, or until tender.

2 Heat the remaining oil in a large frying pan and add the spinach leaves. Cook over a medium heat for 2–3 minutes, until the leaves are just wilted. Season with salt and pepper and divide between the squash halves.

3 Top with the Gorgonzola and return to the oven for 10 minutes, or until the cheese has melted. Season with ground black pepper and serve.

4 acorn squash

250g/9oz baby spinach leaves, washed

200g/7oz Gorgonzola cheese, sliced

FROM THE STORECUPBOARD

45ml/3 tbsp garlic-infused olive oil

salt and ground black pepper

Teriyaki Salmon

Bottles of teriyaki sauce – a lovely rich Japanese glaze – are available in most large supermarkets and Asian stores. Serve the salmon with sticky rice or soba noodles.

SERVES FOUR

4 salmon fillets, 150g/5oz each

75ml/5 tbsp teriyaki marinade

5cm/2in piece of fresh root ginger, peeled and cut into matchsticks

FROM THE STORECUPBOARD

150ml/¹/₄ pint/²/₃ cup sunflower oil

1 Put the salmon in a shallow, non-metallic dish and pour over the teriyaki marinade. Cover and chill for 2 hours.

2 Meanwhile, heat the sunflower oil in a small pan and add the ginger. Fry for 1–2 minutes, or until golden and crisp. Remove with a slotted spoon and drain on kitchen paper.

3 Heat a griddle pan until smoking hot. Remove the salmon from the marinade and add, skin side down, to the pan. Cook for 2–3 minutes, then turn over and cook for a further 1–2 minutes, or until cooked through. Remove from the pan and divide among four serving plates. Top the salmon fillets with the crispy fried ginger.

4 Pour the marinade into the pan and cook for 1–2 minutes. Pour over the salmon and serve.

Roast Mackerel with Spicy Chermoula Paste

Chermoula is a spice mix used widely in Moroccan and North African cooking. It is now readily available in most large supermarkets.

SERVES FOUR

4 whole mackerel, cleaned and gutted

2–3 tbsp chermoula

2 red onions, sliced

FROM THE STORECUPBOARD

75ml/5 tbsp olive oil

salt and freshly ground black pepper

1 Preheat the oven to 190°C/375°F/Gas 5. Place each mackerel on a large sheet of baking parchment. Using a sharp knife, slash each fish several times.

2 In a small bowl, mix the chermoula with the olive oil, and spread over the mackerel, rubbing the mixture into the cuts.

3 Scatter the red onions over the mackerel, and season with salt and pepper. Scrunch the ends of the paper together to seal the fish and place on a baking tray. Bake for 20 minutes, until the mackerel is cooked through. Serve in the paper parcels, to be unwrapped at the table.

Tandoori Chicken

If you have time, prepare this dish when you get up in the morning, so that it's ready to cook for supper. Serve with a red onion and cucumber salad and warmed naan bread.

SERVES FOUR

4 skinless chicken breast fillets and 4 skinless chicken thigh fillets

200ml/7fl oz/scant 1 cup Greek (US strained plain) yogurt

45ml/3 tbsp tandoori curry paste

FROM THE STORECUPBOARD

salt and ground black pepper

1 Using a sharp knife, slash the chicken breasts and thighs and place in a shallow, non-metallic dish.

2 Put the curry paste and yogurt in a bowl and mix together. Season with salt and pepper, then pour over the chicken and toss to coat well. Cover the dish with clear film (plastic wrap) and chill for at least 8 hours.

3 Preheat the oven to 190°C/375°F/Gas 5. Remove the clear film from the chicken and transfer the dish to the oven. Bake for 20–30 minutes, or until the chicken is cooked through. Serve immediately.

Roast Chicken with Black Pudding and Sage

The combination of juicy roast chicken and black pudding is wonderful. Serve as part of a Sunday roast or simply with a salad.

SERVES FOUR

1 medium oven-ready chicken

115g/4oz black pudding (blood sausage), skinned

30ml/2 tbsp fresh sage leaves

FROM THE STORECUPBOARD

25g/1oz/2 tbsp softened butter

salt and ground black pepper

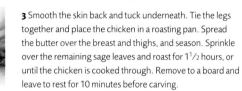

1 Preheat the oven to 190°C/375°F/Gas 5. Carefully push your fingers between the skin and the flesh at the neck end of the bird to loosen it, making sure you don't tear the skin.

2 Shape the black pudding into a flat, roundish shape, to fit the space between the skin and the breast meat. Push it under the skin with half the sage leaves.

3 Smooth the skin back and tuck underneath. Tie the legs together and place the chicken in a roasting pan. Spread the butter over the breast and thighs, and season. Sprinkle over the remaining sage leaves and roast for $1^{1}/_{2}$ hours, or until the chicken is cooked through. Remove to a board and leave to rest for 10 minutes before carving.

Sticky Glazed Pork Ribs

These spare ribs have a lovely sweet-and-sour flavour and are always as popular with children as they are with adults, making them the perfect choice for a family meal. They're also great for cooking over a barbecue; make sure you leave them to marinate for at least 30 minutes before cooking. To enjoy sticky ribs at their best you need to get stuck in and eat them with your fingers, so make sure you serve them with plenty of paper napkins.

SERVES FOUR

1 Preheat the oven to 190°C/375°F/Gas 5. Put the spare ribs in a roasting pan and season well with plenty of salt and ground black pepper.

2 In a small bowl, mix together the honey and soy sauce and pour over the ribs. Turn the ribs several times, spooning over the mixture until thoroughly coated.

3 Bake the spare ribs for 30 minutes, then increase the oven temperature to 220°C/425°F/Gas 7 and cook for a further 10 minutes, or until the honey and soy sauce marinade turns into a thick, sticky glaze.

900g/2lb pork spare ribs

75ml/5 tbsp clear honey

75ml/5 tbsp light soy sauce

FROM THE STORECUPBOARD

salt and ground black pepper

Chinese Spiced Pork Chops

Five-spice powder is a fantastic ingredient for perking up dishes and adding a good depth of flavour. The five different spices – Szechuan pepper, cinnamon, cloves, fennel seeds and star anise – are perfectly balanced, with the aniseed flavour of star anise predominating. Serve the chops with lightly steamed pak choi (bok choy) and plain boiled rice.

SERVES FOUR

4 large pork chops, about 200g/7oz each

15ml/1 tbsp Chinese five-spice powder

30ml/2 tbsp soy sauce

FROM THE STORECUPBOARD

30ml/2 tbsp garlic-infused olive oil

1 Arrange the pork chops in a single layer in a non-metallic roasting pan or baking dish.

2 Sprinkle the five-spice powder over the chops, then drizzle over the soy sauce and garlic infused oil. (Alternatively, mix together the garlic-infused olive oil, soy sauce and five-spice powder, and pour over the chops.)

3 Using your hands, rub the mixture into the meat. Cover the dish with clear film (plastic wrap) and chill for 2 hours.

4 Preheat the oven to 160°C/325°F/Gas 3. Uncover the dish and bake for 30–40 minutes, or until the pork is cooked through and tender. Serve immediately.

Roast Pork with Juniper Berries and Bay

Juniper berries have a strong, pungent taste and are a great flavouring for rich, fatty meats such as pork, while bay leaves add a lovely aroma. Serve with roast potatoes and lightly cooked leafy green vegetables.

SERVES FOUR TO SIX

1kg/2¼lb boned leg of pork

5 fresh bay leaves

6 juniper berries

FROM THE STORECUPBOARD

15ml/1 tbsp olive oil

salt and ground black pepper

1 Preheat the oven to 180°C/350°F/Gas 4. Open out the pork and season with plenty of salt and black pepper.

2 Lay the bay leaves on the pork and sprinkle over the juniper berries. Carefully roll up the pork to enclose the bay leaves and juniper berries and tie with string to secure.

3 Rub the skin with the oil and then rub in plenty of salt. Roast the pork for 20 minutes per 450g/1lb, plus an extra 20 minutes.

4 Remove the pork from the oven and leave to rest for about 10 minutes before carving, then serve immediately.

Lamb Chops with a Mint Jelly Crust

Mint and lamb are classic partners, and the breadcrumbs used here add extra texture. Serve the chops with sweet potatoes baked in their skins and some steamed green vegetables.

SERVES FOUR

1 Preheat the oven to 190°C/375°F/Gas 5. Place the lamb chops on a baking sheet and season with plenty of salt and ground black pepper.

2 Put the breadcrumbs and mint jelly in a bowl and mix together to combine. Spoon the breadcrumb mixture on top of the chops, pressing down firmly with the back of a spoon making sure they stick to the chops.

3 Bake the chops for 20–30 minutes, or until they are just cooked through. Serve immediately.

8 lamb chops, about 115g/4oz each

50g/2oz/1 cup fresh white breadcrumbs

30ml/2 tbsp mint jelly

FROM THE STORECUPBOARD

salt and ground black pepper

Roast Shoulder of Lamb with Whole Garlic Cloves

The potatoes catch the lamb fat as it cooks, giving garlicky, juicy results. Return the potatoes to the oven to keep warm while you leave the lamb to rest before carving. Serve with seasonal vegetables.

SERVES FOUR TO SIX

675g/1¹/₂lb waxy potatoes, peeled and cut into large dice

12 garlic cloves, unpeeled

1 whole shoulder of lamb

FROM THE STORECUPBOARD

45ml/3 tbsp olive oil

salt and ground black pepper

1 Preheat the oven to 180°C/350°F/Gas 4. Put the potatoes and garlic cloves into a large roasting pan and season with salt and pepper. Pour over 30ml/2 tbsp of the oil and toss the potatoes and garlic to coat.

2 Place a rack over the roasting pan, so that it is not touching the potatoes. Place the lamb on the rack and drizzle over the remaining oil. Season with salt and pepper.

3 Roast the lamb and potatoes for 2–2¹/₂ hours, or until the lamb is cooked through. Halfway through the cooking time, carefully take the lamb and the rack off the roasting pan and turn the potatoes to ensure even cooking.

Roast Leg of Lamb with Rosemary and Garlic

This is a classic combination of flavours, and always popular. Serve as a traditional Sunday lunch with roast potatoes and vegetables. Leaving the lamb to rest before carving ensures a tender result.

SERVES FOUR TO SIX

1 leg of lamb, approx 1.8kg/4lb

2 garlic cloves, finely sliced

leaves from 2 sprigs of
fresh rosemary

FROM THE STORECUPBOARD

30ml/2 tbsp olive oil

salt and ground black pepper

1 Preheat the oven to 190°C/375°F/Gas 5. Using a small sharp knife, make slits at 4cm/1¹/₂in intervals over the lamb, deep enough to hold a piece of garlic. Push the garlic and rosemary leaves into the slits.

2 Drizzle the olive oil over the top of the lamb and season with plenty of salt and ground black pepper. Roast for 25 minutes per 450g/1lb of lamb, plus another 25 minutes.

3 Remove the lamb from the oven and leave to rest for about 15 minutes before carving.

Meatballs in Tomato Sauce

Cook meatballs in their sauce, rather than frying them first, because this helps keep them nice and moist. Serve in the traditional way with spaghetti and shavings of Parmesan cheese.

SERVES FOUR

1 Put the minced beef in a bowl and season with salt and pepper. Remove the sausages from their skins and mix thoroughly into the beef.

2 Shape the mixture into balls about the size of large walnuts and arrange in a single layer in a shallow baking dish. Cover and chill for 30 minutes.

3 Preheat the oven to 180°C/350°F/Gas 4. Process the tomatoes in a food processor until just smooth, and season. Pour over the meatballs, making sure they are all covered.

4 Bake the meatballs for 40 minutes, stirring once or twice until they are cooked through, then serve.

225g/8oz/1 cup minced (ground) beef

4 Sicilian-style sausages

2 x 400g/14oz cans pomodorino tomatoes

FROM THE STORECUPBOARD

salt and ground black pepper

Beef Cooked in Red Wine

Shin of beef is traditionally a quite tough cut that needs long, slow cooking, and marinating the beef in red wine gives a tender result. Sprinkle the stew with rosemary and serve with mashed potatoes.

SERVES FOUR TO SIX

675g/1¹/₂lb boned and cubed shin of beef

3 large garlic cloves, finely chopped

1 bottle fruity red wine

FROM THE STORECUPBOARD

salt and ground black pepper

1 Put the beef in a casserole dish with the garlic and some black pepper, and pour over the red wine. Stir to combine, then cover and chill for at least 12 hours.

2 Preheat the oven to 160°C/325°F/Gas 3. Cover the casserole with a tight-fitting lid and transfer to the oven. Cook for 2 hours, or until the beef is very tender. Season with salt and pepper to taste, and serve piping hot.

VARIATION *Marinate the beef in a mixture of half port and half beef stock instead of the red wine. Port cooks down to produce a lovely rich sauce, but be sure to dilute it with stock because it can be quite overpowering on its own. A half-and-half mixture will give the perfect balance of taste.*

On the Side

OFTEN, WHEN YOU'VE COOKED A FABULOUS MAIN
DISH, YOU WANT TO SERVE EQUALLY IMAGINATIVE
ACCOMPANIMENTS BUT JUST DON'T HAVE THE TIME OR
ENERGY. THIS CHAPTER OFFERS THE PERFECT SOLUTION
WITH A WHOLE RANGE OF SIDE DISHES THAT WILL ADD
THE FINISHING TOUCH TO ANY MEAL. THERE'S EVERY
ACCOMPANIMENT YOU COULD ASK FOR, FROM SIMPLE
SALADS AND SPEEDY STIR-FRIED VEGETABLES TO ROAST
POTATOES AND AROMATIC RICE AND NOODLES.

Green Beans with Almond Butter and Lemon

The mild flavour of the almonds in this dish makes it a perfect accompaniment for baked or grilled oily fish such as trout or mackerel.

SERVES FOUR

350g/12oz green beans, trimmed

50g/2oz/¹/₃ cup whole blanched almonds

grated rind and juice of 1 unwaxed lemon

FROM THE STORECUPBOARD

50g/2oz/¹/₄ cup butter

salt and ground black pepper

1 Cook the beans in a pan of salted boiling water for about 3 minutes, or until just tender. Drain well. Meanwhile, melt the butter in a large frying pan until foamy.

2 Add the almonds to the pan and cook, stirring occasionally, for 2–3 minutes, or until golden. Remove from the heat and toss with the beans, lemon rind and juice, and season.

VARIATION This salad is delicious made with different types of nuts. Use the same quantity of roughly chopped shelled walnuts or blanched hazelnuts in place of the almonds.

Garlicky Green Salad with Raspberry Dressing

Adding a splash of raspberry vinegar to the dressing enlivens a simple green salad, turning it into a sophisticated side dish.

SERVES FOUR

1 Heat the oil in a small pan and add the garlic. Fry gently for 1–2 minutes, or until just golden, being careful not to burn the garlic. Remove the garlic with a slotted spoon and drain on kitchen paper. Pour the oil into a small bowl.

2 Arrange the salad leaves in a serving bowl. Whisk the raspberry vinegar into the reserved oil and season with salt and ground black pepper.

3 Pour the garlic dressing over the salad leaves and toss to combine. Sprinkle over the fried garlic slices and serve.

2 garlic cloves, finely sliced

4 handfuls of green salad leaves

15ml/1 tbsp raspberry vinegar

FROM THE STORECUPBOARD

45ml/3 tbsp olive oil

salt and ground black pepper

Minty Broad Beans with Lemon

Young, tender broad beans have a sweet, mild taste and are delicious served in a simple salad. Take advantage of them when they're in season and make them into this fresh, zesty dish. Green peas – either fresh or frozen – are also delicious served in the same way, but you don't need to peel off their already tender skins.

SERVES FOUR

450g/1lb broad (fava) beans, thawed if frozen

grated rind and juice of 1 unwaxed lemon

1 small bunch of fresh mint, roughly chopped

FROM THE STORECUPBOARD

30ml/2 tbsp garlic-infused olive oil

salt and ground black pepper

1 Using your fingers, slip the grey skins off the broad beans and discard – this takes a little time but the result is well worthwhile. Cook the beans in salted boiling water for 3–4 minutes, or until just tender.

2 Drain well and toss with the oil, lemon rind and juice, and mint. Season with salt and pepper, and serve immediately.

COOK'S TIP *When using fresh broad beans, it is easier to cook them first, then run them under cold water before slipping off their skins. Quickly blanch the skinned beans in boiling water to re-heat them.*

Gingered Carrot Salad

This fresh and zesty salad is ideal served as an accompaniment to simple grilled chicken or fish. Some food processors have an attachment that can be used to cut the carrots into batons, which makes quick work of the preparation, but even cutting them by hand doesn't take too long. Fresh root ginger goes perfectly with sweet carrots, and the tiny black poppy seeds not only add taste and texture, but also look stunning against the bright orange of the carrots.

SERVES FOUR

350g/12oz carrots, peeled and cut into fine matchsticks

2.5cm/1in piece of fresh root ginger, peeled and grated

15ml/1 tbsp poppy seeds

FROM THE STORECUPBOARD

30ml/2 tbsp garlic-infused olive oil

salt and ground black pepper

1 Put the carrots in a bowl and stir in the oil and grated ginger. Cover and chill for at least 30 minutes, to allow the flavours to develop.

2 Season the salad with salt and pepper to taste. Stir in the poppy seeds just before serving.

VARIATION *To make a parsnip and sesame seed salad, replace the carrots with parsnips and blanch in boiling salted water for 1 minute before combining with the oil and ginger. Replace the poppy seeds with the same quantity of sesame seeds.*

Roast Asparagus
with Crispy Prosciutto

Choose tender, fine asparagus for this recipe, as it cooks through quickly in the oven without losing its flavour or texture.

SERVES FOUR

350g/12oz fine asparagus spears, trimmed

1 small handful of fresh basil leaves

4 prosciutto slices

FROM THE STORECUPBOARD

30ml/2 tbsp olive oil

salt and ground black pepper

1 Preheat the oven to 190°C/375°F/Gas 5. Put the asparagus in a roasting pan and drizzle with the olive oil. Sprinkle over the basil and season with salt and ground black pepper. Gently stir to coat in the oil, then spread the asparagus in a single layer.

2 Lay the slices of prosciutto on top of the asparagus and cook for 10–15 minutes, or until the prosciutto is crisp and the asparagus is just tender. Serve immediately.

Orange and Chicory Salad with Walnuts

Chicory and oranges are both winter ingredients, so this salad is perfect for serving with hearty winter meat dishes. Blood oranges look especially attractive served in this dish.

SERVES FOUR

2 chicory (Belgian endive) heads

2 oranges

25g/1oz/2 tbsp walnut halves, roughly chopped

FROM THE STORECUPBOARD

30ml/2 tbsp extra virgin olive oil

salt and ground black pepper

1 Trim off the bottom of each chicory head and separate the leaves. Arrange on a serving platter.

2 Place one of the oranges on a chopping board and slice off the top and bottom to expose the flesh. Sit the orange upright and, using a small sharp knife, slice down between the skin and the flesh. Do this all the way around until the orange is completely free of peel and pith. Repeat with the second orange, reserving any juice. Arrange the segments on the platter with the chicory.

3 Whisk the oil with any juice from the oranges, and season with salt and pepper. Sprinkle the walnuts over the salad, drizzle over the dressing and serve.

Stir-fried Broccoli with Soy Sauce and Sesame Seeds

Purple sprouting broccoli has been used for this recipe, but when it is not available an ordinary variety of broccoli, such as calabrese, will also work very well.

SERVES TWO

225g/8oz purple sprouting broccoli

15ml/1 tbsp soy sauce

15ml/1 tbsp toasted sesame seeds

FROM THE STORECUPBOARD

15ml/1 tbsp olive oil

salt and ground black pepper

1 Using a sharp knife, cut off and discard any thick stems from the broccoli and cut the broccoli into long, thin florets.

2 Heat the olive oil in a wok or large frying pan and add the broccoli. Stir-fry for 3–4 minutes, or until tender, adding a splash of water if the pan becomes too dry.

3 Add the soy sauce to the broccoli, then season with salt and ground black pepper to taste. Add sesame seeds, toss to combine and serve immediately.

Stir-fried Brussels Sprouts with Bacon and Caraway Seeds

This is a great way of cooking Brussels sprouts, helping to retain their sweet flavour and crunchy texture. Stir-frying guarantees that there will not be a single soggy sprout in sight, which is often what puts people off these fabulous vegetables.

SERVES FOUR

1 Using a sharp knife, cut the Brussels sprouts into fine shreds and set aside. Heat the oil in a wok or large frying pan and add the bacon. Cook for 1–2 minutes, or until the bacon is beginning to turn golden.

2 Add the shredded sprouts to the wok or pan and stir-fry for 1–2 minutes, or until lightly cooked.

3 Season the sprouts with salt and ground black pepper to taste and stir in the caraway seeds. Cook for a further 30 seconds, then serve immediately.

450g/1lb Brussels sprouts, trimmed and washed

2 streaky (fatty) bacon rashers (strips), finely chopped

10ml/2 tsp caraway seeds, lightly crushed

FROM THE STORECUPBOARD

30ml/2 tbsp sunflower oil

salt and ground black pepper

Cheesy Creamy Leeks

This is quite a rich accompaniment that could easily be served as a meal in itself with brown rice or couscous. Cheddar cheese has been used here for a slightly stronger flavour, but you could use a milder Swiss cheese, such as Gruyère, if you like.

SERVES 4

4 large leeks or 12 baby leeks, trimmed and washed

150ml/¹/₄ pint/²/₃ cup double (heavy) cream

75g/3oz mature Cheddar or Monterey Jack cheese, grated

FROM THE STORECUPBOARD

15ml/1 tbsp olive oil

salt and ground black pepper

1 Preheat the grill (broiler) to high. If using large leeks, slice them lengthways. Heat the oil in a large frying pan and add the leeks. Season with salt and pepper and cook for about 4 minutes, stirring occasionally, until starting to turn golden.

2 Pour the cream into the pan and stir until well combined. Allow to bubble gently for a few minutes.

3 Preheat the grill (broiler). Transfer the creamy leeks to a shallow ovenproof dish and sprinkle with the cheese. Grill for 4–5 minutes, or until the cheese is golden brown and bubbling and serve immediately.

Creamy Polenta with Dolcelatte

Soft-cooked polenta is a tasty accompaniment to meat dishes and makes a delicious change from the usual potatoes or rice. It can also be enjoyed on its own as a hearty snack.

SERVES FOUR TO SIX

900ml/1¹/₂ pints/3³/₄ cups milk

115g/4oz/1 cup instant polenta

115g/4oz Dolcelatte cheese

FROM THE STORECUPBOARD

60ml/4 tbsp extra virgin olive oil

salt and ground black pepper

1 Pour the milk into a large pan and bring to the boil, then add a good pinch of salt. Remove the pan from the heat and pour in the polenta in a slow, steady stream, stirring constantly to combine.

2 Return the pan to a low heat and simmer gently, stirring constantly, for 5 minutes. Remove the pan from the heat and stir in the olive oil.

3 Spoon the polenta into a serving dish and crumble the cheese over the top. Season with more ground black pepper and serve immediately.

Spicy Potato Wedges

These potato wedges are so easy to make and can be served on their own with a garlic mayonnaise dip or as an accompaniment to meat or fish dishes. To make extra-spicy potato wedges, use chilli powder instead of paprika.

SERVES FOUR

675g/1¹/₂lb floury potatoes, such as Maris Piper

10ml/2 tsp paprika

5ml/1 tsp ground cumin

FROM THE STORECUPBOARD

45ml/3 tbsp olive oil

salt and ground black pepper

1 Preheat the oven to 190°C/375°F/Gas 5. Using a sharp knife, cut the potatoes into chunky wedges and place in a roasting pan.

2 In a small bowl, combine the olive oil with the paprika and cumin and season with plenty of salt and ground black pepper. Pour the mixture over the potatoes and toss well to coat thoroughly.

3 Spread the potatoes in a single layer in the roasting pan and bake for 30–40 minutes, or until golden brown and tender. Serve immediately.

Crisp and Golden Roast Potatoes with Goose Fat and Garlic

Goose fat gives the best flavour to roast potatoes and is now widely available in cans in supermarkets. However, if you can't find goose fat, or you want to make a vegetarian version of these potatoes, use a large knob (pat) of butter or 15ml/1 tbsp olive oil instead. If you like, add a couple of bay leaves to the potatoes before roasting; they impart a lovely flavour.

SERVES FOUR

675g/1¹/₂lb floury potatoes, such as Maris Piper, peeled

30ml/2 tbsp goose fat

12 garlic cloves, unpeeled

FROM THE STORECUPBOARD

salt and ground black pepper

1 Preheat the oven to 190°C/375°F/Gas 5. Cut the potatoes into large chunks and cook in a pan of salted, boiling water for 5 minutes. Drain well and give the colander a good shake to fluff up the edges of the potatoes. Return the potatoes to the pan and place it over a low heat for 1 minute to steam off any excess water.

2 Meanwhile, spoon the goose fat into a roasting pan and place in the oven until hot, about 5 minutes. Add the potatoes to the pan with the garlic and turn to coat in the fat. Season well with salt and ground black pepper and roast for 40–50 minutes, turning occasionally, until the potatoes are golden and tender.

Persian Baked Rice

In this Persian-style dish, rice is cooked slowly over a low heat so that a crust forms on the bottom. The mild flavours of saffron and almonds go perfectly together. This dish is an ideal accompaniment for lamb.

SERVES FOUR

450g/1lb basmati rice

a good pinch of saffron strands

50g/2oz/¹/₂ cup flaked (sliced) almonds

FROM THE STORECUPBOARD

50g/2oz/¹/₄ cup butter

salt and ground black pepper

1 Cook the rice in a pan of boiling salted water for 5 minutes, then drain thoroughly. Meanwhile, put the saffron in a small bowl with 30ml/2 tbsp warm water and leave to infuse for at least 5 minutes.

2 Heat the butter in a large flameproof pan and add the almonds. Cook over a medium heat for 2–3 minutes, or until golden, stirring occasionally. Add the rice and stir well, then stir in the saffron and its liquid, plus 1 litre/1³/₄ pints/ 4 cups water. Season and cover with a tight-fitting lid.

3 Cook over a very low heat for 30 minutes, or until the rice is tender and a crust has formed on the bottom of the pan. Fork up the rice to mix in the crust before serving.

Noodles with Sesame - roasted Spring Onions

You can use any kind of noodles for this Asian-style dish. Rice noodles look and taste particularly good, but egg noodles work very well too. Serve with fish and chicken dishes.

SERVES FOUR

1 bunch of spring onions
(scallions), trimmed

225g/8oz flat rice noodles

30ml/2 tbsp oyster sauce

FROM THE STORECUPBOARD

30ml/2 tbsp sesame oil

salt and ground black pepper

1 Preheat the oven to 200ºC/400ºF/Gas 6. Cut the spring onions into three pieces, then put them in a small roasting pan and season with salt and pepper.

2 Drizzle the sesame oil over the spring onions and roast for 10 minutes, until they are slightly charred and tender. Set aside.

3 Cook the noodles according to the instructions on the packet and drain thoroughly. Toss with the spring onions and oyster sauce, and season with ground black pepper. Serve immediately.

Al Fresco

EATING OUTSIDE, WHETHER IT'S A PICNIC, A FAMILY
LUNCH IN THE GARDEN OR A BARBECUE, IS ONE OF THE
GREAT PLEASURES OF SUMMER. THERE'S SOMETHING
QUINTESSENTIALLY RELAXING ABOUT EATING OUT IN
THE OPEN AND THIS CHAPTER IS PACKED WITH SIMPLE,
NO-FUSS RECIPES THAT ARE PERFECT FOR HOT, LAZY
DAYS AND BALMY EVENINGS. TAKE A SELECTION OF
SALADS, MAIN DISHES AND BREADS AND LET EVERYONE
HELP THEMSELVES.

Butter Bean, Tomato and Red Onion Salad

Serve this salad with toasted pitta bread for a fresh summer lunch, or as an accompaniment to meat cooked on a barbecue.

SERVES FOUR

2 x 400g/14oz cans butter (lima) beans, rinsed and drained

4 plum tomatoes, roughly chopped

1 red onion, finely sliced

FROM THE STORECUPBOARD

45ml/3 tbsp herb-infused olive oil

salt and ground black pepper

1 Mix together the beans, tomatoes and onion in a large bowl. Season with salt and pepper, and stir in the oil.

2 Cover the bowl with clear film (plastic wrap) and chill for 20 minutes before serving.

VARIATIONS
- To make a tasty tuna salad, drain a 200g/7oz can tuna, flake the flesh and stir into the bean salad.
- For extra flavour and colour, stir in a handful of pitted black olives and a handful of chopped fresh parsley.
- To make a wholesome version of the Italian salad Panzanella, tear half a loaf of ciabatta into bite-size pieces and stir into the salad. Leave to stand for 20 minutes before serving.

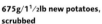

Potato, Caraway Seed and Parsley Salad

Leaving the potatoes to cool in garlic-infused oil with the caraway seeds helps them to absorb plenty of flavour.

SERVES FOUR TO SIX

675g/1¹/₂lb new potatoes, scrubbed

15ml/1 tbsp caraway seeds, lightly crushed

45ml/3 tbsp chopped fresh parsley

FROM THE STORECUPBOARD

45ml/3 tbsp garlic-infused olive oil

salt and ground black pepper

1 Cook the potatoes in salted, boiling water for about 10 minutes, or until just tender. Drain thoroughly and transfer to a large bowl.

2 Stir the oil, caraway seeds and some salt and pepper into the hot potatoes, then set aside to cool. When the potatoes are almost cold, stir in the parsley and serve.

VARIATION
This recipe is also delicious made with sweet potatoes instead of new potatoes. Peel and roughly chop the sweet potatoes, then follow the recipe as before.

Warm Halloumi and Fennel Salad

The firm texture of halloumi cheese makes it perfect for the barbecue, as it keeps its shape very well. It is widely available in most large supermarkets and Greek delicatessens.

SERVES FOUR

200g/7oz halloumi cheese, thickly sliced

2 fennel bulbs, trimmed and thinly sliced

30ml/2 tbsp roughly chopped fresh oregano

FROM THE STORECUPBOARD

45ml/3 tbsp lemon-infused olive oil

salt and ground black pepper

1 Put the halloumi, fennel and oregano in a bowl and drizzle over the lemon-infused oil. Season with salt and black pepper to taste. (Halloumi is a fairly salty cheese, so be very careful when adding extra salt.)

2 Cover the bowl with clear film (plastic wrap) and chill for about 2 hours to allow the flavours to develop.

3 Place the halloumi and fennel on a griddle pan or over the barbecue, reserving the marinade, and cook for about 3 minutes on each side, until charred.

4 Divide the halloumi and fennel among four serving plates and drizzle over the reserved marinade. Serve immediately.

Pear and Blue Cheese Salad

A juicy variety of pear, such as a Williams, is just perfect in this dish. You can use any other blue cheese, such as Stilton or Gorgonzola, in place of the Roquefort if you prefer.

SERVES FOUR

1 Cut the pears into quarters and remove the cores. Thinly slice each pear quarter and arrange on a serving platter.

2 Slice the Roquefort as thinly as possible and place over the pears. Mix the oil and vinegar together and drizzle over the pears. Season with salt and pepper and serve.

COOK'S TIP *Rich, dark balsamic vinegar has an intense yet mellow flavour. It is produced in Modena in the north of Italy and is widely available in most supermarkets.*

4 ripe pears

115g/4oz Roquefort cheese

15ml/1 tbsp balsamic vinegar

FROM THE STORECUPBOARD

30ml/2 tbsp olive oil

salt and ground black pepper

Fresh Crab Sandwiches

There's not much to beat the taste of freshly cooked crab, but if you can't face dealing with live crabs, buy fresh cooked ones. Serve the crab meat with a bowl of rocket and let everyone get in a mess cracking open the claws and making their own sandwiches.

SERVES SIX

3 live crabs, about 900g/ 2lb each

1 crusty wholegrain loaf, sliced

2 lemons, cut into quarters

FROM THE STORECUPBOARD

butter, for spreading

salt and ground black pepper

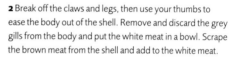

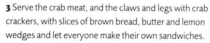

1 Lower the live crabs into a pan of cold water, then slowly bring to the boil. (This method is considered more humane than plunging the crabs into boiling water.) Cook the crabs for 5–6 minutes per 450g/1lb, then remove from the pan and set aside to cool.

2 Break off the claws and legs, then use your thumbs to ease the body out of the shell. Remove and discard the grey gills from the body and put the white meat in a bowl. Scrape the brown meat from the shell and add to the white meat.

3 Serve the crab meat, and the claws and legs with crab crackers, with slices of brown bread, butter and lemon wedges and let everyone make their own sandwiches.

Warm Pasta with Crushed Tomatoes and Basil

It doesn't matter which type of pasta you use for this recipe – any kind you have in the storecupboard will work well.

SERVES FOUR

6 small ripe tomatoes, halved

a small handful of fresh basil leaves

450g/1lb dried pasta shapes

FROM THE STORECUPBOARD

45ml/3 tbsp extra virgin olive oil

salt and ground black pepper

1 Put the halved tomatoes in a bowl and, using your hands, gently squash them until the juices start to run freely. Stir in the olive oil and tear in the basil leaves.

2 Season the tomatoes with salt and pepper and mix well to combine. Cover the bowl with clear film (plastic wrap) and chill for 2–3 hours, to allow the flavours to develop.

3 Remove the tomatoes from the refrigerator and allow them to return to room temperature.

4 Meanwhile, cook the pasta according to the instructions on the packet. Drain well, toss with the crushed tomato and basil mixture and serve immediately.

Roast Shallot Tart
with Thyme

Tarts are perfect for a summer lunch or picnic, and sheets of
ready-rolled puff pastry make tart-making incredibly easy.

SERVES FOUR

**450g/1lb shallots, peeled
and halved**

**30ml/2 tbsp fresh thyme
leaves**

**375g/13oz packet ready-rolled
puff pastry, thawed if frozen**

FROM THE STORECUPBOARD

25g/1oz/2 tbsp butter

salt and ground black pepper

1 Preheat the oven to 190°C/375°F/Gas 5. Heat the butter
in a large frying pan until foaming, then add the shallots.
Season with salt and pepper and cook over a gentle heat for
10–15 minutes, stirring occasionally, until golden. Stir in the
thyme, then remove from the heat and set aside.

2 Unroll the puff pastry on to a large baking sheet. Using a
small, sharp knife, score a border all the way around, about
2.5cm/1in from the edge, without cutting all the way
through the pastry.

3 Spread the shallots over the pastry, inside the border. Bake
for 20–25 minutes, or until the pastry is golden and risen
around the edges. Cut into squares and serve hot or warm.

Roasted Aubergines with Feta and Coriander

Aubergines take on a lovely smoky flavour when grilled on a barbecue. Choose a good quality Greek feta cheese for the best flavour.

SERVES SIX

3 medium aubergines (eggplant)

400g/14oz feta cheese

a small bunch of coriander (cilantro), roughly chopped

FROM THE STORECUPBOARD

60ml/4 tbsp extra virgin olive oil

salt and ground black pepper

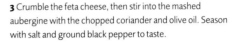

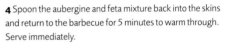

1 Prepare a barbecue. Cook the aubergines for 20 minutes, turning occasionally, until charred and soft. Remove from the barbecue and cut in half lengthways.

2 Carefully scoop the aubergine flesh into a bowl, reserving the skins. Mash the flesh roughly with a fork.

3 Crumble the feta cheese, then stir into the mashed aubergine with the chopped coriander and olive oil. Season with salt and ground black pepper to taste.

4 Spoon the aubergine and feta mixture back into the skins and return to the barbecue for 5 minutes to warm through. Serve immediately.

Barbecued Sardines with Orange and Parsley

Sardines are ideal for the barbecue – the meaty flesh holds together, the skin crisps nicely and there are no lingering indoor cooking smells. Serve them with a selection of salads.

SERVES SIX

6 whole sardines, gutted

1 orange, sliced

a small bunch of fresh flat leaf parsley, chopped

FROM THE STORECUPBOARD

60ml/4 tbsp extra virgin olive oil

salt and ground black pepper

1 Arrange the sardines and orange slices in a single layer in a shallow, non-metallic dish. Sprinkle over the chopped parsley and season with salt and pepper.

2 Drizzle the olive oil over the sardines and orange slices and gently stir to coat well. Cover the dish with clear film (plastic wrap) and chill for 2 hours.

3 Meanwhile, prepare the barbecue. Remove the sardines and orange slices from the marinade and cook the fish over the barbecue for 7–8 minutes on each side, until cooked through. Serve immediately.

Soy Sauce and Star Anise Chicken

The pungent flavour of star anise penetrates the chicken breasts and adds a wonderful aniseedy kick to the smoky flavour of the barbecue. Serve with a refreshing salad.

SERVES FOUR

1 Put the chicken breast fillets in a shallow, non-metallic dish and add the star anise.

2 In a small bowl, whisk together the oil and soy sauce and season with black pepper to make a marinade.

3 Pour the marinade over the chicken and stir to coat each breast fillet all over. Cover the dish with clear film (plastic wrap) and chill for up to 8 hours.

4 Prepare a barbecue. Remove the chicken breasts from the marinade and cook for 8–10 minutes on each side, spooning over the marinade from time to time, until the chicken is cooked through. Serve immediately.

4 skinless chicken breast fillets

2 whole star anise

30ml/2 tbsp soy sauce

FROM THE STORECUPBOARD

45ml/3 tbsp olive oil

ground black pepper

Harissa-spiced Koftas

Serve these spicy koftas in pitta breads with sliced tomatoes, cucumber and mint leaves, with a drizzle of natural yogurt.

SERVES FOUR

450g/1lb/2 cups minced (ground) lamb

1 small onion, finely chopped

10ml/2 tsp harissa paste

FROM THE STORECUPBOARD

salt and ground black pepper

1 Place eight wooden skewers in a bowl of cold water and leave to soak for at least 10 minutes.

2 Put the lamb in a large bowl and add the onion and harissa. Mix well to combine, and season with plenty of salt and ground black pepper.

3 Using wet hands, divide the mixture into eight equal pieces and press onto the skewers in a sausage shape to make the koftas.

4 Prepare a barbecue. Cook the skewered koftas for about 10 minutes, turning occasionally, until cooked through. Serve immediately.

Cumin- and Coriander-rubbed Lamb

Rubs are quick and easy to prepare and can transform everyday cuts of meat such as chops into exciting and more unusual meals. Serve with a chunky tomato salad.

SERVES FOUR

30ml/2 tbsp ground cumin

30ml/2 tbsp ground coriander

8 lamb chops

FROM THE STORECUPBOARD

30ml/2 tbsp olive oil

salt and ground black pepper

1 Mix together the cumin, coriander and oil, and season with salt and pepper. Rub the mixture all over the lamb chops, then cover and chill for 1 hour.

2 Prepare a barbecue. Cook the chops for 5 minutes on each side, until lightly charred but still pink in the centre.

VARIATION *To make ginger- and garlic-rubbed pork, use pork chops instead of lamb chops and substitute the cumin and coriander with ground ginger and garlic granules. Increase the cooking time to 7–8 minutes each side.*

Traditional Irish Soda Bread

Irish soda bread contains no yeast and therefore does not need to be left to rise, so it is quick and easy to make. It is best eaten on the day that it is made, preferably while still warm. You can bake a loaf in the morning, ready to take on a picnic to serve with cheese and salads.

SERVES FOUR TO SIX

450g/1lb plain wholemeal (all-purpose whole-wheat) flour

10ml/2 tsp bicarbonate of soda (baking soda)

400ml/14fl oz/1²/₃ cups buttermilk

FROM THE STORECUPBOARD

5ml/1 tsp salt

1 Preheat the oven to 200°C/400°F/Gas 6. Place the flour in a large bowl and stir in the bicarbonate of soda and salt. Make a well in the centre.

2 Gradually pour the buttermilk into the well, beating in the flour from around the edges to form a soft, not sticky, dough.

3 Turn the dough out on to a lightly floured surface and knead for 5 minutes, until smooth. Shape into a 20cm/8in round and place on a lightly greased baking sheet.

4 Using a sharp knife, cut a deep cross on the top of the dough and bake for 30–35 minutes, or until slightly risen and cooked through. Cool slightly on a wire rack before serving.

Spring Onion Flatbreads

Use these flatbreads to wrap around barbecue-cooked meat and chunky vegetable salads, or serve with tasty dips such as hummus. They're at their best as soon as they're cooked.

MAKES SIXTEEN

1 Place the flour in a large mixing bowl and stir in the salt, yeast and spring onions. Make a well in the centre and pour in 300ml/¹/₂ pint/1¹/₄ cups hand hot water. Mix to form a soft, but not sticky, dough.

2 Turn out the dough on to a floured work surface and knead for about 5 minutes, until smooth. Put the dough back in the bowl, cover with a damp dishtowel and leave in a warm place until doubled in size.

3 Knock back (punch down) the dough to get rid of any excess air and turn out on to a floured work surface. Divide the dough into 16 pieces and roll each piece into a smooth ball. Roll out each ball to a 13cm/5in round.

4 Heat a large frying pan until hot. Dust off any excess flour from one dough round and place in the frying pan. Cook for about 1 minute, then flip over and cook for a further 30 seconds. Repeat with the remaining dough rounds.

450g/1lb/4 cups strong white bread flour, plus extra for dusting

7g/¹/₄ oz packet easy-blend (rapid-rise) dried yeast

4 spring onions (scallions), finely chopped

FROM THE STORECUPBOARD

5ml/1 tsp salt

VARIATION *To make garlic flatbreads, use 2 finely chopped garlic cloves in place of the chopped spring onions. To add extra bite, mix in 1 finely chopped fresh red chilli as well.*

Entertaining

WHEN YOU HAVE INVITED FRIENDS OR FAMILY TO A
SPECIAL MEAL, YOU WANT TO BE ABLE TO SIT BACK AND
ENJOY YOURSELF AS MUCH AS EVERYONE ELSE. THIS
CHAPTER IS PACKED WITH FABULOUS DISHES FOR
EVERY OCCASION – FROM A RELAXED EVENING IN WITH
FRIENDS TO A FORMAL DINNER PARTY. BECAUSE EACH
RECIPE USES SO FEW INGREDIENTS, YOU WON'T NEED
TO SPEND HOURS SHOPPING AND PREPARING – AND
WHEN YOUR GUESTS ARRIVE YOU'LL BE RELAXED,
UNFLUSTERED, AND READY TO ENJOY YOURSELF.

Marinated Smoked Salmon with Lime and Coriander

If you want an elegant appetizer that is really quick to put together, then this is the one for you. The tangy lime juice and aromatic coriander leaves contrast perfectly with the delicate yet distinct flavour of the salmon. Serve with thinly sliced brown bread and butter.

SERVES SIX

200g/7oz smoked salmon

a handful of fresh coriander (cilantro) leaves

grated rind and juice of 1 lime

FROM THE STORECUPBOARD

15ml/1 tbsp extra virgin olive oil

ground black pepper

1 Using a sharp knife or pair of kitchen scissors, cut the salmon into strips and arrange on a serving platter.

2 Sprinkle the coriander leaves and lime rind over the salmon and squeeze over the lime juice. Drizzle with the olive oil and season with black pepper. Cover with clear film (plastic wrap) and chill for 1 hour before serving.

COOK'S TIP *You can make this dish up to 1 hour before serving. However, do not leave it for longer than this because the lime juice will discolour the salmon and spoil the look of the dish.*

Blinis with Caviar and Crème Fraîche

Classic Russian blinis are made with buckwheat flour, which gives them a very distinctive taste. They are available ready-made in large supermarkets and make a tasty first course or snack to serve with drinks, topped with crème fraîche and caviar. Caviar is expensive, but a very small amount goes a long way and the exquisite flavour is well worth it.

SERVES TWELVE

1 Put the crème fraîche in a bowl and season with salt and ground black pepper to taste. Place a teaspoonful of the mixture on each blini.

2 Top each spoonful of crème fraîche with a teaspoon of caviar and serve immediately.

VARIATION *For a stunning effect, top half the blinis with orange salmon or trout roe and the other half with black caviar.*

200g/7oz/scant 1 cup crème fraîche

12 ready-made blinis

60ml/4 tbsp caviar

FROM THE STORECUPBOARD

salt and ground black pepper

Bocconcini with Fennel and Basil

These tiny balls of mozzarella are best when they're perfectly fresh. They should be milky and soft when you cut into them. Buy them from an Italian delicatessen or a good cheese shop.

SERVES SIX

1 Drain the bocconcini well and place in a bowl. Stir in the olive oil, fennel seeds and basil, and season with salt and pepper. Cover and chill for 1 hour.

2 Remove the bowl from the refrigerator and leave to stand for about 30 minutes for the cheese to return to room temperature before serving.

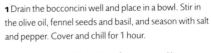

COOK'S TIP *Bocconcini are mini mozzarella balls, each one hand-stretched and rolled, then preserved in brine. If you can't find bocconcini, use ordinary mozzarella cut into bitesize pieces.*

450g/1lb bocconcini mozzarella

5ml/1 tsp fennel seeds, lightly crushed

a small bunch of fresh basil leaves, roughly torn

FROM THE STORECUPBOARD

45ml/3 tbsp extra virgin olive oil

salt and ground black pepper

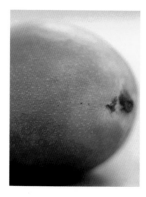

Thai-style Rare Beef and Mango Salad

This simplified version of Thai beef salad is especially tasty served with little bowls of fresh coriander (cilantro) leaves, chopped spring onions (scallions) and peanuts for sprinkling at the table.

SERVES FOUR

450g/1lb sirloin steak

45ml/3 tbsp soy sauce

2 mangoes, peeled (pitted), stoned and finely sliced

FROM THE STORECUPBOARD

45ml/3 tbsp garlic-infused olive oil

ground black pepper

1 Put the steak in a shallow, non-metallic dish and pour over the oil and soy sauce. Season with pepper and turn the steaks to coat in the marinade. Cover and chill for 2 hours.

2 Heat a griddle pan until hot. Remove the steak from the marinade and place on the griddle pan. Cook for 3–5 minutes on each side, moving the steak halfway through if you want a criss-cross pattern.

3 Transfer the steak to a board and leave to rest for 5–10 minutes. Meanwhile, pour the marinade into the pan and cook for a few seconds, then remove from the heat. Thinly slice the steak and arrange on four serving plates with the mangoes. Drizzle over the pan juices to serve.

Wild Mushroom and Fontina Tart

Use any types of wild mushrooms you like in this tart – chanterelles, morels, horns of plenty and ceps all have wonderful flavours. It makes an impressive vegetarian main course, served with a green salad.

SERVES SIX

225g/8oz ready-made shortcrust pastry, thawed if frozen

350g/12oz/5 cups mixed wild mushrooms, sliced if large

150g/5oz Fontina cheese, sliced

FROM THE STORECUPBOARD

50g/2oz/¹/₄ cup butter

salt and ground black pepper

1 Preheat the oven to 190°C/375°F/Gas 5. Roll out the pastry and use to a line a 23cm/9in loose-bottomed flan tin (tart pan). Chill the pastry for 30 minutes, then bake blind for 15 minutes. Set aside.

2 Heat the butter in a large frying pan until foaming. Add the mushrooms and season with salt and ground black pepper. Cook over a medium heat for 4–5 minutes, moving the mushrooms about and turning them occasionally with a wooden spoon, until golden.

3 Arrange the mushrooms in the cooked pastry case with the Fontina. Return the tart to the oven for 10 minutes, or until the cheese is golden and bubbling. Serve hot.

Parmigiana di Melanzane

This flavoursome Italian dish can be served as a vegetarian main course, or as an accompaniment to meat or chicken dishes. For a delicious variation, layer a few artichoke hearts between the slices of aubergine.

SERVES EIGHT

900g/2lb aubergines (eggplant), sliced lengthways

600ml/1 pint/2¹/₂ cups garlic and herb passata (bottled strained tomatoes)

115g/4oz/1¹/₄ cups freshly grated Parmesan cheese

FROM THE STORECUPBOARD

60ml/4 tbsp olive oil

salt and ground black pepper

1 Preheat the grill (broiler) to high. Brush the aubergine slices with the oil and season with salt and pepper to taste. Arrange them in a single layer on a grill pan and grill (broil) for 4–5 minutes on each side, until golden and tender. (You will have to do this in batches.)

2 Preheat the oven to 190°C/375°F/Gas 5. Spoon a little passata into a large baking dish. Arrange a single layer of aubergine slices over the top and sprinkle with some grated Parmesan cheese. Repeat the layers of passata, aubergine and Parmesan until all the ingredients have been used up, finishing with a good sprinkling of Parmesan. Bake for 20–25 minutes, or until golden and bubbling.

Pan-fried Skate Wings with Capers

This sophisticated way of serving skate is perfect for a dinner party. Serve with a light, green salad.

SERVES SIX

1 Heat the butter in a large frying pan and add one of the skate wings. Fry for 4–5 minutes on each side, until golden and cooked through.

2 Using a fish slice (metal spatula) carefully transfer the cooked skate wing to a warmed serving plate and keep warm while you cook each of the remaining skate wings in the same way.

3 Return the pan to the heat and add the lime rind and juice, and capers. Season with salt and freshly ground black pepper to taste and allow to bubble for 1–2 minutes. Spoon a little of the juices and the capers over each skate wing and serve immediately.

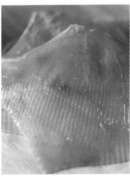

6 small skate wings

grated rind and juice of 2 limes

30ml/2 tbsp salted capers, rinsed and drained

FROM THE STORECUPBOARD

50g/2oz/^{1}/$_{4}$ cup butter

salt and ground black pepper

Sea Bass with Parsley and Lime Butter

The delicate but firm, sweet flesh of sea bass goes beautifully with citrus flavours. Serve with roast fennel and sautéed diced potatoes.

SERVES SIX

6 sea bass fillets, about 150g/5oz each

grated rind and juice of 1 large lime

30ml/2 tbsp chopped fresh parsley

FROM THE STORECUPBOARD

50g/2oz/¹/₄ cup butter

salt and ground black pepper

1 Heat the butter in a large frying pan and add three of the sea bass fillets, skin side down. Cook for 3–4 minutes, or until the skin is crisp and golden. Flip the fish over and cook for a further 2–3 minutes, or until cooked through.

2 Remove the fillets from the pan with a metal spatula. Place each on a serving plate and keep them warm. Cook the remaining fish in the same way and transfer to serving plates.

3 Add the lime rind and juice to the pan with the parsley, and season with salt and black pepper. Allow to bubble for 1–2 minutes, then pour a little over each fish portion and serve immediately.

Mussels in White Wine

This simple yet delicious dish is perfect for informal entertaining. Serve with a big bowl of chips (US fries) to share. To make a variation, cook the mussels in beer instead of wine – they taste fantastic.

SERVES TWO

300ml/¹/₂ pint/1¹/₄ cups dry white wine

1kg/2¹/₄lb mussels, cleaned

45ml/3 tbsp chopped fresh parsley

FROM THE STORECUPBOARD

25g/1oz/2 tbsp butter

salt and ground black pepper

1 Heat the butter in a large pan until foaming, then pour in the wine. Bring to the boil. Discard any open mussels that do not close when sharply tapped, and add the remaining ones to the pan. Cover with a tight-fitting lid and cook over a medium heat for 4–5 minutes, shaking the pan every now and then. By this time, all the mussels should have opened. Discard any that are still closed.

2 Line a large sieve with kitchen paper and strain the mussels and their liquid through it. Transfer the mussels to warmed serving bowls. Pour the liquid into a small pan and bring to the boil. Season with salt and pepper and stir in the parsley. Pour over the mussels and serve immediately.

Pot-roasted Chicken with Preserved Lemons

Roasting chicken and potatoes in this way gives an interesting variety of textures. The chicken and potatoes on the top crisp up, while underneath they stay soft and juicy. Serve with steamed carrots or curly kale.

SERVES FOUR TO SIX

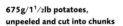

675g/1¹/₂lb potatoes, unpeeled and cut into chunks

6–8 pieces of preserved lemon

1.3kg/3lb corn-fed chicken, jointed

FROM THE STORECUPBOARD

30ml/2 tbsp olive oil

salt and ground black pepper

1 Preheat the oven to 190°C/375°F/Gas 5. Drizzle the olive oil into the bottom of a large roasting pan. Spread the chunks of potato in a single layer in the pan and tuck in the pieces of preserved lemon.

2 Pour about 1cm/¹/₂in of cold water into the roasting pan. Arrange the chicken pieces on top and season with plenty of salt and black pepper. Roast for 45 minutes–1 hour, or until the chicken is cooked through, and serve.

Chilli-spiced Poussin

When you are short of time these spicy poussins make a quick alternative to a traditional roast. Serve with a leafy salad.

SERVES FOUR

2 poussins, 675g/1¹/₂lb each

15ml/1 tbsp chilli powder

15ml/1 tbsp ground cumin

FROM THE STORECUPBOARD

45ml/3 tbsp olive oil

salt and ground black pepper

1 Spatchcock one poussin: remove the wishbone and split the bird along each side of the backbone and remove it. Press down on the breastbone to flatten the bird. Push a metal skewer through the wings and breast to keep the bird flat, then push a second skewer through the thighs and breast. Spatchcock the second poussin in the same way.

2 Combine the chilli, cumin, oil and seasoning. Brush over the poussins. Preheat the grill (broiler). Lay the birds, skin side down, on a grill rack and grill (broil) for 15 minutes. Turn over and grill for a further 15 minutes until cooked through.

3 Remove the skewers and split each bird in half along the breastbone. Serve drizzled with the pan juices.

Roast Pheasant with Sherry and Mustard Sauce

Use only young pheasants for roasting – older birds are too tough and only suitable for casseroles. Serve with potatoes braised in wine with garlic and onions, Brussels sprouts and bread sauce.

SERVES FOUR

2 young oven-ready pheasants

200ml/7fl oz/scant 1 cup sherry

15ml/1 tbsp Dijon mustard

FROM THE STORECUPBOARD

50g/2oz/¹/₄ cup softened butter

salt and ground black pepper

1 Preheat the oven to 200°C/400°F/Gas 6. Put the pheasants in a roasting pan and spread the butter all over both birds. Season with salt and pepper.

2 Roast the pheasants for 50 minutes, basting often to stop the birds from drying out. When the pheasants are cooked, take them out of the pan and leave to rest on a board, covered with foil.

3 Meanwhile, place the roasting pan over a medium heat. Add the sherry and season with salt and pepper. Simmer for 5 minutes, until the sherry has slightly reduced, then stir in the mustard. Carve the pheasants and serve with the sherry and mustard sauce.

Marmalade and Soy Roast Duck

Sweet-and-sour flavours, such as marmalade and soy sauce, complement the rich, fatty taste of duck beautifully. Serve these robustly flavoured duck breast portions with simple accompaniments such as steamed sticky rice and lightly cooked pak choi (bok choi).

SERVES SIX

6 duck breast portions

45ml/3 tbsp fine-cut marmalade

45ml/3 tbsp light soy sauce

FROM THE STORECUPBOARD

salt and ground black pepper

1 Preheat the oven 190°C/375°F/Gas 5. Place the duck breasts skin side up on a grill (broiler) rack and place in the sink. Pour boiling water all over the duck. This shrinks the skin and helps it crisp during cooking. Pat the duck dry with kitchen paper and transfer to a roasting pan.

2 Combine the marmalade and soy sauce, and brush over the duck. Season with a little salt and some black pepper and roast for 20–25 minutes, basting occasionally with the marmalade mixture in the pan.

3 Remove the duck breasts from the oven and leave to rest for 5 minutes. Slice the duck breasts and serve drizzled with any juices left in the pan.

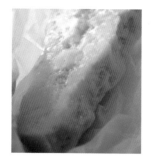

Porchetta

This is a simplified version of a traditional Italian festive dish. Make sure the piece of belly pork has a good amount of crackling – because this is the best part, which guests will just love. Serve with creamy mashed potatoes and a green vegetable.

SERVES EIGHT

2kg/4¹/₂lb boned belly pork

45ml/3 tbsp fresh rosemary leaves, roughly chopped

50g/2oz/²/₃ cup freshly grated Parmesan cheese

FROM THE STORECUPBOARD

15ml/1 tbsp olive oil

salt and ground black pepper

1 Preheat the oven to 180°C/350°F/Gas 4. Lay the belly pork skin side down on a board. Spread the rosemary leaves over the meat and sprinkle with the grated Parmesan cheese. Season with salt and freshly ground black pepper and drizzle over the olive oil.

2 Starting from one end, roll the pork up firmly and tie string around it at 2.5cm/1in intervals, to secure. Transfer the rolled pork to a roasting pan and cook for about 3 hours, or until cooked through.

3 Transfer the pork to a board and leave to rest for about 10 minutes, then carve into slices and serve immediately.

Sweet-and-sour Lamb

Buy lamb loin chops from your butcher and ask him to French trim them for you. Serve with steamed carrots or green beans.

SERVES FOUR

8 French-trimmed lamb loin chops

90ml/6 tbsp balsamic vinegar

30ml/2 tbsp caster (superfine) sugar

FROM THE STORECUPBOARD

30ml/2 tbsp olive oil

salt and ground black pepper

1 Put the lamb chops in a shallow, non-metallic dish and drizzle over the balsamic vinegar. Sprinkle with the sugar and season with salt and black pepper. Turn the chops to coat in the mixture, then cover with clear film (plastic wrap) and chill for 20 minutes.

2 Heat the olive oil in a large frying pan and add the chops, reserving the marinade. Cook for 3–4 minutes on each side.

3 Pour the marinade into the pan and leave to bubble for about 2 minutes, or until reduced slightly. Remove from the pan and serve immediately.

Roast Lamb with Figs

Lamb fillet is an expensive cut of meat, but because it is very lean there is very little waste. To make a more economical version of this dish, use leg of lamb instead. It has a stronger flavour but is equally good. Serve with steamed green beans.

SERVES SIX

1kg/2¹/₄lb lamb fillet

9 fresh figs

150ml/¹/₄ pint/²/₃ cup ruby port

FROM THE STORECUPBOARD

30ml/2 tbsp olive oil

salt and ground black pepper

1 Preheat the oven to 190°/375°F/Gas 5. Heat the oil in a roasting pan over a medium heat. Add the lamb fillet and sear on all sides until evenly browned.

2 Cut the figs in half and arrange around the lamb. Season the lamb with salt and ground black pepper and roast for 30 minutes. Pour the port over the figs.

3 Return the lamb to the oven and roast for a further 30–45 minutes. The meat should still be slightly pink in the middle so be careful not to overcook.

4 Transfer the lamb to a board and leave to rest for about 5 minutes. Carve into slices and serve.

Cookies and Simple Desserts

SOMETIMES ONLY SOMETHING SWEET WILL DO. FROM
COOKIES AND CAKES TO REALLY SIMPLE DESSERTS, THIS
CHAPTER IS PACKED WITH LOVELY IDEAS TO TANTALIZE
THE TASTEBUDS. WHEN BAKING AND DESSERT-MAKING
IS THIS SIMPLE, WHY MAKE DO WITH STORE-BOUGHT
COOKIES AND CAKES OR READY-MADE DESSERTS AND
ICE CREAM? MAKE YOUR OWN AND REALLY ENJOY THE
PLEASURE OF A HOME-MADE TREAT.

Rich Butter Cookies

These crunchy, buttery cookies make a delicious afternoon treat served with a cup of tea or a glass of milk. The dough can be made in advance and chilled until you are ready to bake the cookies.

MAKES TWENTY-FIVE TO THIRTY

90g/3¹/₂oz/¹/₂ cup golden caster (superfine) sugar

250g/9oz/2¹/₄ cups plain (all-purpose) flour

demerara (raw) sugar, for coating

FROM THE STORECUPBOARD

175g/6oz/³/₄ cup unsalted (sweet) butter, at room temperature, diced

1 Put the butter and sugar in a bowl and beat until light and fluffy. Add the flour and gradually work it in. Knead until smooth, then roll into a sausage shape about 30cm/12in long, then pat the sides flat to form a square log.

2 Sprinkle a thick layer of demerara sugar on a piece of baking parchment. Press each side of the dough into the sugar to coat. Wrap and chill for 30 minutes, or until firm. Meanwhile, preheat the oven to 160°C/325°F/Gas 3.

3 Remove the dough from the refrigerator and unwrap. Cut into thick slices and place slightly apart on non-stick baking sheets. Bake the cookies for 20 minutes, or until just beginning to turn brown. Transfer to a wire rack to cool.

Almond Macaroons

These giant macaroons are crisp on the outside, chewy in the middle, and are perfect for anyone on a gluten- or dairy-free diet. Ground almonds can be a tasty alternative to the wheat flour used in most cookies, and macaroons don't need butter for their deliciously moist, rich taste.

MAKES NINE

2 egg whites

115g/4oz/1 cup ground almonds

130g/4¹⁄₂oz/generous ¹⁄₂ cup light muscovado (brown) sugar

1 Preheat the oven to 180°C/350°F/Gas 4. Line a large baking sheet with baking parchment. Using an electric whisk, whisk the egg whites in a large, clean bowl until they form stiff peaks.

2 Sprinkle the ground almonds and sugar over the beaten egg whites, and gently fold in using a large metal spoon.

3 Place nine spoonfuls of the mixture on the baking sheet, spacing them well apart, and flatten them slightly with the back of the spoon. Bake the macaroons for 15 minutes, or until risen, deep golden and beginning to turn crisp.

4 Leave the macaroons on the baking sheets for about 5 minutes to firm up slightly. Using a metal spatula, carefully transfer to a wire rack to cool completely.

Chocolate Crispy Cookies

These little chocolate-coated cornflake cookies are always a great hit with kids. Roll their edges in icing (confectioners') sugar before serving.

MAKES TEN

1 Line a large baking sheet with baking parchment. Put the chocolate and syrup in a heatproof bowl placed over a pan of simmering water and stir until melted.

2 Put the cornflakes in a plastic bag and, using a rolling pin, lightly crush them. Remove the chocolate mixture from the heat and add the cornflakes. Mix until thoroughly combined.

3 Place a 6cm/2^1/$_2$in round cutter on the baking parchment and put a spoonful of the chocolate mixture in the centre. Pack down firmly with the spoon to make a thick cookie. Ease away the cutter, using the spoon to keep the mixture in place. Continue making cookies in this way until all the mixture has been used up. Cover and chill for at least 1 hour before serving.

90g/3^1/$_2$oz milk chocolate, broken into squares

15ml/1 tbsp golden (light corn) syrup

90g/3^1/$_2$oz/4^1/$_2$ cups cornflakes

Meringue Squiggles

These delightful meringue wands are easy to make, taste delicious and look fantastic. They're popular with children and adults alike and are great as a teatime treat or as a simple dessert with ice cream.

MAKES FOURTEEN TO SIXTEEN

1 Preheat the oven to 150°C/300°F/Gas 2. Line a large baking sheet with baking parchment. Put the egg whites in a large bowl, reserving about 15ml/1 tbsp for decoration, and whisk until they form firm peaks. Add a spoonful of caster sugar and whisk briefly to combine. Add another spoonful and whisk again. Continue in this way until all the sugar has been incorporated.

2 Spoon the meringue mixture into a large piping (pastry) bag fitted with a large plain nozzle. Pipe wavy lines of meringue, about 13cm/5in long, on to the baking sheet and bake for about 1 hour, or until dry and crisp.

3 Carefully peel the meringues off the paper and transfer to a wire rack to cool. Using a fine pastry brush, brush the tops of the meringues with the reserved egg white, then scatter over the multi-coloured sugar sprinkles to decorate.

2 egg whites

90g/3¹/₂oz/¹/₂ cup caster (superfine) sugar

multi-coloured sugar sprinkles, to decorate

COOK'S TIP

If you prefer not to use raw egg white to decorate the meringue squiggles, use a sugar paste instead. Put 45ml/ 3 tbsp icing (confectioners') sugar in a small bowl and add a few drops of water. Stir well to make a paste, then brush on to the meringues.

Chocolate and Prune Refrigerator Bars

Wickedly self-indulgent and very easy to make, these fruity chocolate bars will keep for 2–3 days in the refrigerator – if they don't all get eaten as soon as they are ready.

MAKES TWELVE BARS

250g/9oz good quality milk chocolate

115g/4oz digestive biscuits (graham crackers)

115g/4oz/^{1}/$_2$ cup ready-to-eat prunes

FROM THE STORECUPBOARD

50g/2oz/^{1}/$_4$ cup unsalted (sweet) butter

1 Break the chocolate into small pieces and place in a heatproof bowl. Add the butter and melt in the microwave on high for 1–2 minutes. Stir to mix and set aside. (Alternatively, place the bowl over a pan of gently simmering water and leave until melted, stirring frequently.)

2 Put the biscuits in a plastic bag and seal, then bash into small pieces with a rolling pin. Roughly chop the prunes and stir into the melted chocolate with the biscuits.

3 Spoon the chocolate and prune mixture into a 20cm/8in square cake pan and chill for 1–2 hours until set. Remove the cake from the refrigerator and, using a sharp knife, cut into 12 bars and serve.

Blueberry Cake

Cake mixes make life very easy and are available in most supermarkets.
Dust with icing (confectioners') sugar and serve for a simple dessert.

SERVES SIX TO EIGHT

1 Preheat the oven to 190°C/375°F/Gas 5. Grease a 20cm/8in
cake tin (pan). Make up the sponge cake mix according to the
instructions on the packet, using the egg if required. Spoon the
mixture into the prepared cake tin.

2 Bake the cake according to the instructions on the packet.
Ten minutes before the end of the cooking time, sprinkle the
blueberries over the top of the cake. (Work quickly so that the
cake is out of the oven for as short a time as possible, otherwise
it may sink in the middle.)

3 Leave the cake to cool in the tin for 2–3 minutes, then carefully
remove from the tin and transfer to a wire rack. Leave to cool
completely before serving.

**220g/8oz packet sponge
cake mix**

1 egg, if needed

**115g/4oz/1 cup
blueberries**

Pistachio and Rose Water Oranges

This light and citrusy dessert is perfect to serve after a heavy main course, such as a hearty meat stew or a leg of roast lamb. Combining three favourite Middle Eastern ingredients, it is delightfully fragrant and refreshing. If you don't have pistachio nuts, use hazelnuts instead.

SERVES FOUR

1 Slice the top and bottom off one of the oranges to expose the flesh. Using a small serrated knife, slice down between the pith and the flesh, working round the orange, to remove all the peel and pith. Slice the orange into six rounds, reserving any juice. Repeat with the remaining oranges.

2 Arrange the orange rounds on a serving dish. Mix the reserved juice with the rose water and drizzle over the oranges. Cover the dish with clear film (plastic wrap) and chill for about 30 minutes. Sprinkle the chopped pistachio nuts over the oranges to serve.

4 large oranges

30ml/2 tbsp rose water

30ml/2 tbsp shelled pistachio nuts, roughly chopped

COOK'S TIP
Rose-scented sugar is delicious sprinkled over fresh fruit salads. Wash and thoroughly dry a handful of rose petals and place in a sealed container filled with caster (superfine) sugar for 2–3 days. Remove the petals before using the sugar.

Summer Berry Frozen Yogurt

Any combination of summer fruits will work for this dish, as long as they are frozen, because this helps to create a chunky texture. Whole fresh or frozen berries make an attractive decoration.

SERVES SIX

350g/12oz/3 cups frozen summer fruits

200g/7oz/scant 1 cup Greek (US strained plain) yogurt

25g/1oz icing (confectioners') sugar

VARIATION *To make a rich and creamy ice cream, use double (heavy) cream in place of the yogurt. It's a lot less healthy but the taste is irresistible.*

1 Put all the ingredients into a food processor and process until combined but still quite chunky. Spoon the mixture into six 150ml/¼ pint/⅔ cup ramekin dishes.

2 Cover each dish with clear film (plastic wrap) and place in the freezer for about 2 hours, or until firm.

3 To turn out the frozen yogurts, dip the dishes briefly in hot water and invert them on to small serving plates. Tap the base of the dishes and the yogurts should come out. Serve immediately.

Raspberry Sherbet

Traditional sherbets are made in a similar way to sorbets but with added milk. This low-fat version is made from raspberry purée blended with sugar syrup and virtually fat-free fromage frais or yogurt.

SERVES SIX

175g/6oz/scant 1 cup caster (superfine) sugar

500g/1¼lb/3½ cups raspberries, plus extra, to serve

500ml/17fl oz/2 ¼ cups virtually fat-free fromage frais or yogurt

COOK'S TIP *To make the sherbet by hand, pour the raspberry purée into a freezerproof container and freeze for 4 hours, beating once with a fork, electric whisk or in a food processor to break up the ice crystals. Freeze, then beat again.*

1 Put the sugar in a small pan with 150ml/¼ pint/⅔ cup water and bring to the boil, stirring until the sugar has dissolved completely. Pour into a jug (pitcher) and cool.

2 Put 350g/12oz/2½ cups of the raspberries in a food processor and blend to a purée. Press through a sieve into a large bowl and discard the seeds. Stir the sugar syrup into the raspberry purée and chill until very cold.

3 Add the fromage frais or yogurt to the chilled purée and whisk until smooth. Using an ice-cream maker, churn the mixture until it is thick but too soft to scoop. Scrape into a freezerproof container, then crush the remaining raspberries between your fingers and add to the ice cream. Mix lightly then freeze for 2–3 hours until firm. Scoop the ice cream into dishes and serve with extra raspberries.

Pineapple Crush Ice Cream

Look out for pineapples that are labelled "extra sweet". This variety has bright sunflower-yellow flesh that is naturally sweet and juicy. It is ideal for making the most wonderful ice cream.

SERVES FOUR TO SIX

1 Slice one pineapple in half legthwise through the leafy top, then scoop out the flesh from both halves, keeping the shells intact. Stand them upside down to drain, wrap in clear film (plastic wrap) and chill until needed.

2 Trim the top off the remaining pineapple, cut the flesh into slices, then cut away the skin and any eyes. Remove the core from each slice, then finely chop the flesh from both pineapples. Purée 300g/11oz of the pineapple in a food processor or blender, reserving the remaining pineapple.

3 Using an ice-cream maker, churn the pineapple purée with the sugar for 15–20 minutes. Mix in the cream and churn until thick but too soft to scoop.

4 Add 175g/6oz/1¹/₂ cups of the pineapple and continue to churn the ice cream until it is stiff enough to serve in scoops. Serve, offering any remaining pineapple separately.

2 extra-sweet pineapples

50g/2oz/¹/₄ cup caster (superfine) sugar

300ml/¹/₂ pint/1¹/₄ cups whipping cream

VARIATION *This ice cream is also delicious mixed with meringues: crumble four meringue nests into the ice cream mixture when adding the pineapple.*

Chocolate Banana Fools

This de luxe version of banana custard looks great served in glasses. It can be made a few hours in advance and chilled until ready to serve.

SERVES FOUR

1 Put the chocolate in a heatproof bowl and melt in the microwave on high power for 1–2 minutes. Stir, then set aside to cool. (Alternatively, put the chocolate in a heatproof bowl and place it over a pan of gently simmering water and leave until melted, stirring frequently.)

115g/4oz plain (semisweet) chocolate, chopped

300ml/¹/₂ pint/1¹/₄ cups fresh custard

2 bananas

2 Pour the custard into a bowl and gently fold in the melted chocolate to make a rippled effect.

3 Peel and slice the bananas and stir these into the chocolate and custard mixture. Spoon into four glasses and chill for 30 minutes–1 hour before serving.

Lemon Posset

This simple creamy dessert has distant origins, dating back to the Middle Ages. It is perfect for warm summer evenings and is particularly good served with crisp shortbread cookies .

SERVES FOUR

1 Gently heat the cream and sugar together until the sugar has dissolved, then bring to the boil, stirring constantly. Add the lemon juice and rind and stir until the mixture thickens.

2 Pour the mixture into four heatproof serving glasses and chill until just set, then serve.

600ml/1 pint/2¹/₂ cups double (heavy) cream

175g/6oz/scant 1 cup caster (superfine) sugar

grated rind and juice of 2 unwaxed lemons

COOK'S TIP *To make shortbread cookies, put 225g/8oz/1 cup chilled butter in a food processor and add 115g/4oz/ ²/₃ cup caster (superfine) sugar, 225g/ 8oz/2 cups plain (all-purpose) flour and 115g/4oz/²/₃ cup ground rice. Process to form a dough, then shape into a log 5cm/2in wide and wrap in clear film (plastic wrap). Chill for 30 minutes. Preheat the oven to 190°C/ 375°F/Gas 5. Cut the dough into thin slices, and bake for 15–20 minutes.*

Rhubarb and Ginger Trifles

Choose a good quality jar of rhubarb compote for this recipe; try to find one with large, chunky pieces of fruit.

SERVES FOUR

12 gingernut biscuits (gingersnaps)

50ml/2fl oz/$^1/_4$ cup rhubarb compote

450ml/$^3/_4$ pint/scant 2 cups extra thick double (heavy) cream

1 Put the ginger biscuits in a plastic bag and seal. Bash the biscuits with a rolling pin until roughly crushed.

2 Set aside two tablespoons of crushed biscuits and divide the rest among four glasses.

3 Spoon the rhubarb compote on top of the crushed biscuits, then top with the cream. Place in the refrigerator and chill for about 30 minutes.

4 To serve, sprinkle the reserved crushed biscuits over the trifles and serve immediately.

Strawberry Cream Shortbreads

These pretty desserts are always popular. Serve them as soon as they are ready because the shortbread cookies will lose their lovely crisp texture if left to stand.

SERVES THREE

150g/5oz strawberries

450ml/³/₄ pint/scant 2 cups double (heavy) cream

6 round shortbread biscuits (cookies)

VARIATION *You can use any other berry you like for this dessert – try raspberries or blueberries. Two ripe, peeled peaches will also give great results.*

1 Reserve three strawberries for decoration. Hull the remaining strawberries and cut them in half.

2 Put the halved strawberries in a bowl and gently crush using the back of a fork. (Only crush the berries lightly; they should not be reduced to a purée.)

3 Put the cream in a large, clean bowl and whip to form soft peaks. Add the crushed strawberries and gently fold in to combine. (Do not overmix.)

4 Halve the reserved strawberries, then spoon the strawberry and cream mixture on top of the shortbread cookies. Decorate each one with half a strawberry and serve immediately.

Raspberry Brûlée

Cracking through the caramelized sugary top of a crème brûlée to reveal the creamy custard underneath is always so satisfying. These ones have the added bonus of a deliciously rich, fruity custard packed with crushed raspberries.

SERVES FOUR

1 Tip the raspberries into a large bowl and crush with a fork. Add the custard and gently fold in until combined.

2 Divide the mixture between four 120ml/4fl oz/^{1}/$_2$ cup ramekin dishes. Cover each one with clear film (plastic wrap) and chill in the refrigerator for 2–3 hours.

3 Preheat the grill (broiler) to high. Remove the clear film from the ramekin dishes and place them on a baking sheet. Sprinkle the sugar over the custards and grill (broil) for 3–4 minutes, or until the sugar has caramelized.

4 Remove the custards from the grill and set aside for a few minutes to allow the sugar to harden, then serve.

115g/4oz fresh raspberries

300ml/^{1}/$_2$ pint/1^1/$_4$ cups ready-made fresh custard

75g/3oz caster (superfine) sugar

COOK'S TIP

You can now buy little gas blow torches for use in the kitchen. They make quick work of caramelizing the sugar on top of the brûlées – and are also fun to use!

Portuguese Custard Tarts

Called *pastéis de nata* in Portugal, these tarts are traditionally served with a small strong coffee as a sweet breakfast dish, but they are equally delicious served as a pastry or dessert.

MAKES TWELVE

1 Preheat the oven to 200°C/400°F/Gas 6. Roll out the pastry and cut out twelve 13cm/5in rounds. Line a 12-hole muffin tin (pan) with the pastry rounds. Line each pastry round with a circle of baking parchment and some baking beans or uncooked rice.

2 Bake the tarts for 10–15 minutes, or until the pastry is cooked through and golden. Remove the paper and baking beans or rice and set aside to cool.

3 Spoon the custard into the pastry cases and dust with the icing sugar. Place the tarts under a preheated hot grill (broiler) and cook until the sugar caramelizes. Remove from the heat and leave to cool before serving.

225g/8oz ready-made puff pastry, thawed if frozen

175ml/6fl oz/³/₄ cup fresh ready-made custard

30ml/2 tbsp icing (confectioners') sugar

Plum and Almond Tart

To transform this tart into an extravagant dessert, dust with a little icing (confectioners') sugar and serve with a dollop of crème fraîche.

SERVES FOUR

1 Preheat the oven to 190°C/375°F/Gas 5. Unroll the pastry on to a large baking sheet. Using a small, sharp knife, score a border 5cm/2in from the edge of the pastry, without cutting all the way through.

2 Roll out the marzipan into a rectangle, to fit just within the pastry border, then lay it on top of the pastry, pressing down lightly with the tips of your fingers.

3 Scatter the sliced plums on top of the marzipan in an even layer and bake for 20–25 minutes, or until the pastry is risen and golden brown.

4 Carefully transfer the tart to a wire rack to cool slightly, then cut into squares or wedges and serve.

375g/13oz ready-rolled puff pastry, thawed if frozen

115g/4oz marzipan

6–8 plums, stoned and sliced

Baked Apples with Marsala

The Marsala cooks down with the juice from the apples and the butter to make a rich, sticky sauce. Serve these delicious apples with a spoonful of extra-thick cream.

SERVES SIX

1 Preheat the oven to 180°C/350°F/Gas 4. Using an apple corer, remove the cores from the apples and discard.

2 Place the apples in a small, shallow baking pan and stuff the figs into the holes in the centre of each apple.

3 Top each apple with a quarter of the butter and pour over the Marsala. Cover the pan tightly with foil and bake for about 30 minutes.

4 Remove the foil from the apples and bake for a further 10 minutes, or until the apples are tender and the juices have reduced slightly. Serve immediately with any remaining pan juices drizzled over the top.

4 medium cooking apples

50g/2oz/¹/₃ cup ready-to-eat dried figs

150ml/¹/₄ pint/²/₃ cup Marsala

FROM THE STORECUPBOARD

50g/2oz/¹/₄ cup butter, softened

Elegant Desserts

THERE'S NOTHING LIKE A SOPHISTICATED DESSERT
TO FINISH OFF A MEAL, PARTICULARLY WHEN YOU'RE
ENTERTAINING. IF YOU'VE GOT FRIENDS OVER, AND
YOU'VE ALREADY PREPARED A MOUTHWATERING
APPETIZER AND AN AWE-INSPIRING MAIN COURSE,
WHAT YOU REALLY NEED IS A SIMPLE YET SUMPTUOUS
DESSERT. TRY YOUR HAND AT MAKING INDIVIDUAL
LEMON AND RASPBERRY TARTLETS OR ROAST PEACHES
WITH AMARETTO. YOUR GUESTS WILL LOVE THEM AND
NEED NEVER KNOW HOW EASY THEY WERE TO MAKE!

Watermelon Ice

This simple, refreshing dessert is perfect after a hot, spicy meal. The aromatic flavour of kaffir lime leaves goes perfectly with watermelon.

SERVES FOUR TO SIX

90ml/6 tbsp caster (superfine) sugar

4 kaffir lime leaves, torn into small pieces

500g/1¼lb watermelon

1 Put the sugar and lime leaves in a pan with 105ml/7 tbsp water. Heat gently until the sugar has dissolved, then pour into a large bowl and set aside to cool.

2 Cut the watermelon into wedges with a large knife. Cut the flesh from the rind, remove the seeds and chop the flesh. Place the flesh in a food processor and process to a slush, then mix in the sugar syrup. Chill for 3–4 hours.

3 Strain the chilled mixture into a freezer container and freeze for 2 hours, then beat with a fork to break up the ice crystals. Return to the freezer and freeze for 3 hours more, beating at half-hourly intervals, then freeze until firm. Transfer the ice to the refrigerator about 30 minutes before serving.

Coffee Ice Cream

This classic ice cream is always a favourite and, despite its simplicity, has an air of sophistication and elegance about it. If you have an ice cream maker, simply pour the mixture into it and churn until firm.

SERVES EIGHT

1 Put the custard in a large bowl and stir in the coffee. In a separate bowl, whip the cream until soft but not stiff and fold evenly into the coffee and custard mixture.

2 Pour the mixture into a freezerproof container and cover with a tight-fitting lid or clear film (plastic wrap) and freeze for about 2 hours.

600ml/1 pint/2¹/₂ cups fresh ready-made custard

150ml/¹/₄ pint/²/₃ cup strong black coffee

300ml/¹/₂ pint/1¹/₄ cups double (heavy) cream

3 Remove the ice cream from the freezer and beat with a fork to break up the ice crystals.

4 Return the ice cream to the freezer, freeze for a further 2 hours, then beat again. Return it to the freezer until completely frozen, then serve.

Blackberries in Port

Pour this rich fruit compote over ice cream or serve it with a spoonful of clotted cream to create an attractive, rich dessert. It's unbelievably quick and easy to make and is the perfect end to a dinner party. Blackberries can be found growing wild on hedgerows in late summer and there's nothing better than picking them yourself for this lovely dessert.

SERVES FOUR

300ml/¹/₂ pint/1¹/₄ cups ruby port

75g/3oz/6 tbsp caster (superfine) sugar

450g/1lb/4 cups blackberries

1 Pour the port into a pan and add the sugar and 150ml/ ¹/₄ pint/²/₃ cup water. Stir over a gentle heat with a wooden spoon until the sugar has dissolved.

2 Remove the pan from the heat and stir in the blackberries. Set aside to cool, then pour into a bowl and cover with clear film (plastic wrap). Chill until ready to serve.

Baby Summer Puddings

This classic English dessert is always a favourite, and serving it in individual portions with spoonfuls of clotted cream makes it extra special. White bread that is more than a day old actually works better than fresh bread. Slices of brioche make a wonderful alternative to white bread.

SERVES FOUR

6 white bread slices, crusts removed

450g/1lb/4 cups summer fruits

75g/3oz/6 tbsp caster (superfine) sugar

COOK'S TIP *You can enjoy this lovely dessert even in the winter. Use frozen summer fruits, which are available in supermarkets all year round. Simply thaw the fruits, then cook as if using fresh fruits.*

1 Cut out four rounds from the bread slices, large enough to fit in the bottom of four 175ml/6fl oz/³/₄ cup dariole moulds.

2 Line the moulds with clear film (plastic wrap) and place a bread round in the base of each mould. Reserve two slices of bread and cut the remaining bread into slices and use to line the sides of the moulds, pressing to fit.

3 Put the summer fruits in a pan with the sugar and heat gently until the sugar has dissolved. Bring to the boil, then simmer gently for 2–3 minutes. Remove from the heat and leave to cool slightly, then spoon into the moulds.

4 Cut four rounds out of the remaining slices of bread to fit the top of the dariole moulds. Place the bread rounds on the fruit and push down to fit. Cover each dariole mould loosely with clear film and place a small weight on top.

5 Chill the desserts overnight, then turn out on to serving plates. Remove the clear film lining and serve immediately.

Tangy Raspberry and Lemon Tartlets

You can make the pastry cases for these little tartlets in advance and store them in an airtight container until ready to serve.

SERVES FOUR

1 Preheat the oven to 190°C/375°F/Gas 5. Roll out the pastry and use to line four 9cm/3½in tartlet tins (muffin pans). Line each tin with a circle of baking parchment and fill with baking beans or uncooked rice.

2 Bake for 15–20 minutes, or until golden and cooked through. Remove the baking beans or rice and paper and take the pastry cases out of the tins. Leave to cool completely on a wire rack.

3 Set aside 12 raspberries for decoration and fold the remaining ones into the lemon curd. Spoon the mixture into the pastry cases and top with the reserved raspberries. Serve immediately.

175g/6oz ready-made short-crust pastry, thawed if frozen

120ml/8 tbsp good quality lemon curd

115g/4oz/²⁄₃ cup fresh raspberries

Crispy Mango Stacks with Raspberry Coulis

This makes a very healthy yet stunning dessert – it is low in fat and contains no added sugar. However, if the raspberries are a little sharp, you may prefer to add a pinch of sugar to the purée.

SERVES FOUR

3 filo pastry sheets, thawed if frozen

2 small ripe mangoes

115g/4oz/²/₃ raspberries, thawed if frozen

FROM THE STORECUPBOARD

50g/2oz/¹/₄ cup butter, melted

1 Preheat the oven to 200°C/400°F/Gas 6. Lay the filo sheets on a clean work surface and cut out four 10cm/4in rounds from each. Brush each round with the melted butter and lay the rounds on two baking sheets. Bake for 5 minutes, or until crisp and golden. Place on wire racks to cool.

2 Peel the mangoes, remove the stones and cut the flesh into thin slices. Put the raspberries in a food processor with 45ml/3 tbsp water and process to a purée. Place a pastry round on each of four serving plates. Top with a quarter of the mango and drizzle with a little of the raspberry purée. Repeat until all the ingredients have been used, finishing with a layer of mango and a drizzle of raspberry purée.

Cherry Chocolate Brownies

This is a modern version of the classic Black Forest gâteau. Choose really good quality bottled fruits because this will make all the difference to the end result. Look out for bottled fruits at Christmas-time, in particular, when supermarket shelves are packed with different varieties. Other types of fruit will work equally well – try slices of orange bottled in liqueur or pears bottled in brandy.

SERVES FOUR

1 Using a sharp knife, carefully cut the brownies in half crossways to make two thin slices. Place one brownie square on each of four serving plates.

2 Pour the cream into a large bowl and whip until soft but not stiff, then divide half the whipped cream between the four brownie squares.

3 Divide half the cherries among the cream-topped brownies, then place the remaining brownie halves on top of the cherries. Press down lightly.

4 Spoon the remaining cream on top of the brownies, then top each one with more cherries and serve immediately.

4 chocolate brownies

300ml/¹/₂ pint/1¹/₄ cups double (heavy) cream

20–24 bottled cherries in Kirsch

Coffee Mascarpone Creams

For the best results, use good quality coffee beans and make the coffee as strong as possible. These little desserts are very rich so you need a really robust shot of coffee to give the desired result. They are particularly good served with a glass of liqueur or a cup of espresso.

SERVES FOUR

1 Put the Mascarpone in a bowl and add the coffee. Mix well until smooth and creamy. Sift in the icing sugar and stir until thoroughly combined.

2 Spoon the mixture into little china pots or ramekin dishes and chill for 30 minutes before serving.

115g/4oz/¹/₂ cup Mascarpone cheese

45ml/3 tbsp strong espresso coffee

45ml/3 tbsp icing (confectioners') sugar

VARIATION You can flavour Mascarpone with almost anything you like to make a quick but elegant dessert. Try replacing the coffee with the same quantity of orange juice, Marsala or honey.

Deep-fried Cherries

Fresh fruit coated with a simple batter and then deep-fried is delicious and makes an unusual dessert. These succulent cherries are perfect sprinkled with sugar and cinnamon and served with a classic vanilla ice cream.

SERVES FOUR TO SIX

450g/1lb ripe red cherries, on their stalks

225g/8oz batter mix

1 egg

FROM THE STORECUPBOARD

vegetable oil, for deep-frying

1 Gently wash the cherries and pat dry with kitchen paper. Tie the stalks together with fine string to form clusters of four or five cherries.

2 Make up the batter mix according to the instructions on the packet, beating in the egg. Pour the vegetable oil into a deep-fat fryer or large, heavy pan and heat to 190°C/375°F.

3 Working in batches, half-dip each cherry cluster into the batter and then carefully drop the cluster into the hot oil. Fry for 3–4 minutes, or until golden. Remove the deep-fried cherries with a wire-mesh skimmer or slotted spoon and drain on a wire rack placed over crumpled kitchen paper, and serve immediately.

Passion Fruit Soufflés

These simplified soufflés are so easy and work beautifully. The passion fruit adds a tropical note to a favourite classic. The soufflés look very pretty sprinkled with icing (confectioners') sugar.

SERVES FOUR

200ml/7fl oz/scant 1 cup ready-made fresh custard

3 passion fruits, halved

2 egg whites

FROM THE STORECUPBOARD

a knob (pat) of softened butter, for greasing

1 Preheat the oven to 200°C/400°F/Gas 6. Grease four 200ml/7fl oz/scant 1 cup ramekin dishes with the butter.

2 Pour the custard into a large mixing bowl. Scrape out the seeds and juice from the halved passion fruit and stir into the custard until well combined.

3 Whisk the egg whites until stiff, and fold a quarter of them into the custard. Carefully fold in the remaining egg whites, then spoon the mixture into the ramekin dishes.

4 Place the dishes on a baking sheet and bake for 8–10 minutes, or until the soufflés are well risen. Serve immediately.

Roast Peaches with Amaretto

This is an excellent dessert to serve in summer, when peaches are at their juiciest and most fragrant. The apricot and almond flavour of the amaretto liqueur subtly enhances the sweet, fruity taste of ripe peaches. Serve with a spoonful of crème fraîche or whipped cream.

SERVES FOUR

1 Preheat the oven 190°C/375°F/Gas 5. Cut the peaches in half and prise out the stones (pits) with the point of the knife.

2 Place the peaches cut side up in a roasting pan. In a small bowl, mix the amaretto liqueur with the honey, and drizzle over the halved peaches, covering them evenly.

3 Bake the peaches for 20–25 minutes, or until tender. Place two peach halves on each serving plate and drizzle with the pan juices. Serve immediately.

4 ripe peaches

45ml/3 tbsp Amaretto di Sarone liqueur

45ml/3 tbsp clear honey

COOK'S TIP

You can cook these peaches over a barbecue. Place them on sheets of foil, drizzle over liqueur, then scrunch the foil around them to seal. Cook for 15–20 minutes.

Grilled Pineapple and Rum Cream

The sweeter and juicier the pineapple, the more delicious the pan juices will be in this tropical dessert. To test whether the pineapple is ripe, gently pull the green spiky leaves at the top of the fruit. If they come away easily, the fruit is ripe and ready to use.

SERVES FOUR

1 Heat the butter in a frying pan and add the pineapple. Cook over a moderate to high heat until the pineapple is starting to turn golden. Add the rum and allow to bubble for 1–2 minutes. Remove the pan from the heat and set aside to cool completely.

2 Whip the cream until it is soft but not stiff. Fold the pineapple and rum mixture evenly through the cream, then divide it between four glasses and serve.

115g/4oz pineapple, roughly chopped

45ml/3 tbsp dark rum

300ml/¹/₂ pint/1¹/₄ cups double (heavy) cream

FROM THE STORECUPBOARD

25g/1oz/2 tbsp butter

Chocolate Petit Four Cookies

Make these dainty cookies as stylish after-dinner snacks. If you do not have any amaretto liqueur, they will work well without it. Alternatively, you can substitute the same quantity of brandy or rum.

SERVES EIGHT

1 Preheat the oven according to the instructions on the cookie dough packet. Roll out the cookie dough on a floured surface to 1cm/¹/₂in thick. Using a 2.5cm/1in cutter, stamp out as many rounds from the dough as possible and transfer them to a lightly greased baking sheet. Bake for about 8 minutes, or until cooked through. Transfer to a wire rack to cool completely.

2 To make the filling, break the chocolate into small pieces and place in a heatproof bowl with the butter and amaretto liqueur. Sit the bowl over a pan of gently simmering water and stir occasionally, until the chocolate has melted. Remove from the heat and set aside to cool.

3 Spread a small amount of the filling on the flat bottom of one of the cookies and sandwich together with another. Repeat until all the biscuits have been used.

350g/12oz carton chocolate chip cookie dough

115g/4oz plain (semisweet) chocolate

30ml/2 tbsp Amaretto di Sarone liqueur

FROM THE STORECUPBOARD

50g/2oz/¹/₄ cup butter

Praline Chocolate Bites

These delicate, mouthwatering little bites never fail to impress guests, but are quite simple to make. They are perfect for serving with coffee after dinner. Dust with icing sugar for a decorative finish.

SERVES FOUR

1 Put the sugar in a heavy pan with 90ml/6 tbsp water. Stir over a gentle heat until the sugar has dissolved. Bring the syrup to the boil and cook for about 5 minutes, without stirring, until the mixture is golden and caramelized.

2 Remove the pan from the heat and tip in the almonds, swirling the pan to immerse them in the caramel. Tip the mixture on to a lightly oiled baking sheet and set aside for 10–15 minutes, or until hardened. Meanwhile, melt the chocolate in a heatproof bowl set over a pan of simmering water.

3 Cover the hardened caramel mixture with clear film (plastic wrap) and break up with a rolling pin then place in a food processor. Process until finely chopped, then stir into the melted chocolate. Chill until set enough to roll into balls. Roll the mixture into 16 balls and place in mini paper cases to serve.

115g/4oz/1 cup caster (superfine) sugar

115g/4oz/²/₃ cup whole blanched almonds

200g/7oz plain (semisweet) chocolate

COOK'S TIP · *The mixture for these bites can be made ahead and stored in the freezer for up to 2 weeks. To use, thaw the mixture at room temperature until soft enough to roll into balls.*

Drinks

FROM HEALTHY JUICE-BOOSTS TO CHILLED COCKTAILS,
ICY SHAKES AND WINTER WARMERS, THERE ARE MANY
UNUSUAL DRINKS YOU CAN MAKE WITH JUST THREE
INGREDIENTS. YOU'LL NEED A SPECIAL ELECTRIC JUICER
TO MAKE SOME OF THE JUICES BUT ALL THE OTHER
DRINKS CAN BE WHIPPED UP IN AN INSTANT USING
ORDINARY KITCHEN EQUIPMENT. TRY A REFRESHING
GLASS OF GRAPEFRUIT AND PEAR JUICE, OR AN
INDULGENT PEPPERMINT CANDY CRUSH OR WARM
YOURSELF UP WITH A CUP OF CARDAMOM HOT
CHOCOLATE OR A RUM AND STAR ANISE HOT TODDY.

Tomato and Cucumber Juice with Basil

Some herbs don't juice well, losing their aromatic flavour and turning muddy and dull. Basil, on the other hand, is an excellent juicer, keeping its distinctive fresh fragrance. It makes the perfect partner for mild, refreshing cucumber and the ripest, juiciest tomatoes you can find. Try using cherry tomatoes for an extra sweet flavour.

MAKES TWO SMALL GLASSES

¹/₂ cucumber, peeled

a handful of fresh basil

350g/12oz tomatoes

1 Quarter the cucumber lengthways. There's no need to remove the seeds. Push it through a juicer with the basil, then do the same with the tomatoes.

2 Pour the tomato, basil and cucumber juice over ice cubes in one tall or two short glasses and echo the herb flavour by adding a few basil sprigs for decoration.

Beetroot, Ginger and Orange Juice

Despite its firmness, beetroot can be juiced raw and its intense flavour goes perfectly with tangy citrus fruits and fresh root ginger. It has the highest sugar content of any vegetable and makes a delicious juice with a vibrant colour and rich but refreshing taste.

MAKES ONE LARGE GLASS

200g/7oz raw beetroot (beets)

1cm/^{1}/$_2$in piece fresh root ginger, peeled

1 large orange

1 Scrub the beetroot, then trim them and cut into quarters. Push half the beetroot through a vegetable juicer, followed by the ginger and the remaining beetroot and pour the juice into a jug (pitcher).

2 Squeeze the juice from the orange, using a citrus juicer or by hand, and pour into the beetroot juice. Stir to combine.

3 Pour the juice over ice cubes in a glass or clear glass cup and serve immediately to enjoy the full benefit of all the nutrients. (Do not let the ice cubes melt into the juice or they will dilute its flavour.)

Grapefruit and Pear Juice

This deliciously refreshing rose-tinged blend will keep you bright-eyed and bushy-tailed. Its sharp yet sweet flavour is perfect for breakfast or as a pick-me-up when energy levels are flagging. If the grapefruit are particularly tart, serve the juice with a little bowl of brown sugar, or even brown sugar stirrers.

MAKES TWO TALL GLASSES

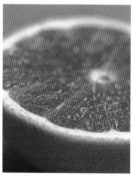

2 pink grapefruit, halved

2 ripe pears

1 Take a thin slice from one grapefruit half and halve it. Cut a few thin slices of pear. Squeeze the juice from the grapefruit halves, then the pears using a juicer.

2 Combine the fruit juices and pour into two glasses. Add a few ice cubes to each glass and decorate with the grapefruit and pear slices. Serve immediately.

Strawberry Apple Slush

Sweet, juicy strawberries make a delicately fragrant juice, with a consistency that's not too thick and not too thin. The addition of apple juice and just a hint of vanilla creates a tantalizing treat that's perfect for sipping on a lazy summer's afternoon.

MAKES TWO TALL GLASSES

300g/11oz/2³/₄ cups ripe strawberries

2 small, crisp eating apples

10ml/2 tsp vanilla syrup

1 Reserve a couple of strawberries and hull the remaining ones. Roughly chop the apples and push all the fruits through a juicer. Stir in the vanilla syrup.

2 Half-fill two tall glasses with crushed ice. Pour over the juice, decorate with the reserved strawberries (slicing them if you like) and serve immediately.

Lavender Orange Lush

This fragrant, lavender-scented juice is guaranteed to perk up a jaded palate in no time at all. It has a heavenly aroma and distinct yet subtle taste. Make plenty and keep it in the refrigerator. Use extra lavender sprigs as fun stirrers or a pretty garnish.

MAKES FOUR TO SIX GLASSES

10–12 lavender flowers

45ml/3 tbsp caster (superfine) sugar

8 large oranges

1 Pull the lavender flowers from their stalks and put them into a bowl with the sugar and 120ml/4fl oz/^{1}/$_2$ cup boiling water. Stir briskly until the sugar has dissolved, then leave the lavender to steep for 10 minutes.

2 Squeeze the oranges using a citrus juicer and pour the juice into a jug (pitcher). Strain the lavender syrup into the juice and chill. Serve poured over ice.

Ice Cool Currant

Intensely flavoured blackcurrants, whizzed in a blender with crushed ice, make a drink so thick and slushy that you might want to serve it with long spoons. If you have a glut of blackcurrants, make a double quantity of the juice and store it in the refrigerator for up to a week, ready to blend with ice.

MAKES TWO TALL GLASSES

125g/4¹/₄oz/generous 1 cup blackcurrants

60ml/4 tbsp light muscovado (brown) sugar

good pinch of mixed (apple pie) spice (optional)

1 Put the blackcurrants and sugar in a pan. (There is no need to string the blackcurrants first.) Add the mixed spice, if using, and pour in 100ml/3¹/₂fl oz/scant ¹/₂ cup water. Bring the mixture to the boil and cook for 2–3 minutes, or until the blackcurrants are completely soft.

2 Press the mixture through a sieve into a bowl, pressing the pulp with the back of a dessertspoon to extract as much juice as possible. Set aside to cool completely.

3 Put 225g/8oz crushed ice in a food processor or blender with the cooled juice and process for about 1 minute until slushy and thoroughly mixed. Scrape the drink into tall glasses and serve immediately.

Cuba Libre

Rum and coke takes on a much livelier, citrus flavour in this vibrant Caribbean cocktail that's sure to put you in the mood to party. The refreshing flavour and aroma of freshly squeezed limes is the dominant taste in this blend, and the dark rum really packs a punch when combined with the sweet, syrupy cola drink.

MAKES EIGHT GLASSES

9 limes

250ml/8fl oz/1 cup dark rum

800ml/1¹/₃ pints/3¹/₂ cups cola drink

1 Thinly slice one lime then, using a citrus juicer, squeeze the juice from the rest of the limes.

2 Put plenty of ice cubes into a large glass jug (pitcher), tucking the lime slices around them, then pour in the lime juice.

3 Pour the rum into the jug and stir well with a long-handled spoon. Top up with cola drink and serve immediately in tall glasses with stirrers.

Blue Lagoon

Blueberries are not only an excellent source of betacarotene and vitamin C, but they are also rich in flavonoids, which help to cleanse the system. Mixed with other dark red fruits, such as blackberries and grapes, they make a highly nutritious and extremely delicious blend that can be stored in the refrigerator and enjoyed throughout the day.

MAKES ONE GLASS

90g/3¹/₂oz/scant 1 cup
blackcurrants
or blackberries

150g/5oz red grapes

130g/4¹/₂oz/generous 1 cup
blueberries

1 If using blackcurrants, gently pull the stalks through the tines of a fork to remove the fruit, then remove the stalks from the grapes.

2 Push all the fruits through a juicer, saving a few for decoration. Place some ice in a medium glass and pour over the juice. Decorate with the reserved fruit and serve.

Lemon Float

Traditional lemonade made with freshly squeezed lemons and served with scoops of ice cream and soda water makes the ultimate refresher. The lemonade can be stored in the refrigerator for up to two weeks, so make a double batch when the weather is hot.

MAKES FOUR LARGE GLASSES

1 Finely grate the rind from the lemons, then squeeze out the juice using a citrus juicer. Put the rind in a bowl with the sugar and pour over 600ml/1 pint/2^1/$_2$ cups boiling water. Stir until the sugar dissolves, then leave to cool.

2 Stir the lemon juice into the cooled syrup. Strain and chill for several hours. To serve, put a scoop of ice cream in each glass, then half-fill with the lemonade and add plenty of lemon slices. Top up with soda water (club soda) and add another scoop of ice cream to each glass and serve immediately.

6 lemons

200g/7oz/1 cup caster (superfine) sugar

8 scoops vanilla ice cream

Tropical Fruit Royale

Based on the Kir Royale, a blend of champagne and crème de cassis, this elegant cocktail is made with tropical fruits and sparkling wine. Remember to blend the fruits ahead of time to give the mango ice cubes time to freeze.

MAKES SIX GLASSES

1 Peel the mangoes, cut the flesh off the stone (pit), then put the flesh in a food processor or blender. Process until smooth, scraping the mixture down from the sides of the bowl.

2 Fill an ice cube tray with a good half of the mango purée and freeze for 2 hours until solid.

3 Cut six wedges from one or two of the passion fruits and scoop the pulp from the rest into the remaining mango purée. Process until well blended.

4 Spoon the mixture into six stemmed glasses. Divide the mango ice cubes among the glasses, top up with sparkling wine and add the passion fruit wedges. Serve with stirrers.

2 large mangoes

6 passion fruit

sparkling wine

Lemon Vodka

Very similar to the deliciously moreish Italian liqueur, Limoncello, this lemon vodka should be drunk in small quantities due to its hefty alcoholic punch. Blend the sugar, lemons and vodka and keep in a bottle in the refrigerator, ready for pouring over crushed ice, or topping up with soda or sparkling water.

MAKES TWELVE TO FIFTEEN GLASSES

10 large lemons

275g/10oz/generous 1¼ cups caster (superfine) sugar

250ml/8fl oz/1 cup vodka

1 Squeeze the lemons using a citrus juicer. Pour the juice into a jug (pitcher), add the sugar and whisk well until all the sugar has dissolved.

2 Strain the sweetened lemon juice into a clean bottle or narrow-necked jar and add the vodka. Shake the mixture well to combine and chill for up to 2 weeks.

3 To serve, fill small glasses with ice and pour over the lemon vodka or pour into larger, ice-filled glasses and top up with chilled soda water (club soda).

Quick Bloody Mary

Using vodka flavoured with chilli gives this drink the perfect spicy kick. You can make your own chilli vodka, simply by slipping a fresh red chilli into a bottle of vodka and leaving the flavours to infuse.

SERVES FOUR

250ml/8fl oz/1 cup chilli vodka

1.2 litres/2 pints/5 cups tomato juice

5ml/1 tsp celery salt

FROM THE STORECUPBOARD

2.5ml/$^1/_2$ tsp ground black pepper

1 Quarter-fill four tall glasses with a handful of ice cubes and pour over the chilli vodka. (If there's a chilli in the bottle, be careful not to pour it out!)

2 Pour the tomato juice into a jug (pitcher) and add the celery salt and pepper. Stir well to combine.

3 Pour the flavoured tomato juice over the vodka, mix well using a long-handled spoon or stirrer, and serve with a stick of celery in each glass.

Peppermint Candy Crush

The next time you see peppermint candy canes that are on sale at Christmas time, buy a few sticks and make this fun kid's drink . All you need to do is whizz up the candy with some milk and freeze until slushy, so it's ready and waiting for thirsty youngsters.

MAKES FOUR GLASSES

90g/3¹/₂oz pink peppermint candy canes, plus four extra to serve

750ml/1¹/₄ pints/3 cups milk

a few drops of pink food colouring (optional)

1 While the candy canes are still in their wrappers, break into small bits using a rolling pin. (If it is unwrapped, put the candy in a polythene bag before you crush it.) Tip the pieces into a food processor or blender.

2 Pour the milk over the candy and add a few drops of pink food colouring, if using. Process until the cane is broken up into tiny pieces, then pour the mixture into a shallow freezer container and freeze for 2 hours, or until frozen around the edges.

3 Beat the mixture with a fork, breaking up the semi-frozen areas and stirring them into the centre. Re-freeze and repeat the process once or twice more until the mixture is slushy. Spoon into tall glasses and serve with candy cane stirrers.

Chocolate Brownie Milkshake

This truly indulgent drink is so simple, yet utterly rich and luxurious, so take a quiet moment to yourself and just sit back, relax and enjoy. For an even more indulgent treat, spoon over whipped cream and sprinkle with grated chocolate to serve.

MAKES ONE LARGE GLASS

40g/1¹/₂oz chocolate brownies

200ml/7fl oz/scant 1 cup full cream (whole) milk

2 scoops vanilla ice cream

1 Crumble the chocolate brownies into a food processor or blender and add the milk. Blend until the mixture is smooth.

2 Add the ice cream to the chocolate milk mixture and blend until the shake is really smooth and frothy. Pour into a tall glass and serve immediately.

Rum and Star Anise Hot Toddy

Hot toddies are normally made with whisky but rum works really well too and produces a deliciously warming drink that's perfect for a cold winter evening – or even a winter afternoon after a hearty walk out in the freezing cold countryside. You can also flavour this toddy with different spices such as a vanilla pod (bean) or cinnamon stick.

SERVES FOUR

300ml/¹/₂ pint/1¹/₄ cups dark rum

45ml/3 tbsp caster (superfine) sugar

1 star anise

1 Pour the rum into a heatproof jug (pitcher) and add the sugar and star anise. Pour in 450ml/³/₄ pint/scant 2 cups boiling water and stir thoroughly until the sugar has dissolved.

2 Carefully pour the hot toddy into heatproof glasses or mugs and serve immediately.

Cardamom Hot Chocolate

Hot chocolate is a wonderful treat at any time of day – for breakfast with a warm croissant, as a teatime treat on a cold winter afternoon or before bed to help you sleep. Adding spicy cardamom gives this hot chocolate an extra rich, fragrant aroma.

SERVES FOUR

900ml/1¹/₂ pints/3³/₄ cups milk

2 cardamom pods, bruised

200g/7oz plain (semisweet) chocolate, broken into pieces

1 Put the milk in a pan with the cardamom pods and bring to the boil. Add the chocolate and whisk until melted.

2 Using a slotted spoon, remove the cardamom pods and discard. Pour the hot chocolate into heatproof glasses, mugs or cups and serve with whipped cream.

Index

chilli-spiced chicken wings, 90
crème fraîche and coriander
  chicken, 124
flavouring, 16
honey mustard chicken, 123
pot-roasted chicken with
  preserved lemons, 191
roast chicken with black pudding
  and sage, 139
soy sauce and star anise
  chicken, 175
stir-fried chicken with red
  peppers and Thai basil, 124
stock, 44
tandoori chicken, 138
chicken livers see liver
chicory: orange and chicory salad
  with walnuts, 155
chillies, 30, 37
broccoli and chilli spaghetti, 109
chilli and spring onion
  noodles, 51
chilli prawn skewers, 89
chilli-rubbed poussin, 192
chilli-spiced chicken wings, 90
fried chilli polenta triangles, 52
grilled hake with lemon and, 122
chilli sauce, 37
chives, 28
smoked salmon and chive
  omelette, 74
chocolate, 35
cardamom hot chocolate, 251
cherry chocolate brownies, 226
chocolate and banana fools, 210
chocolate and prune refrigerator
  bars, 204
chocolate brioche
  sandwiches, 66
chocolate brownie
  milkshake, 249
chocolate crispy cookies, 202
chocolate petit four cookies, 232
praline chocolate bites, 232
sauces, 48
chorizo sausage and spring onion
  hash, 110
cider, pan-fried gammon with, 127
cilantro see coriander
cinnamon, 32
rum and cinnamon cream, 49
citrus fruit, 18
cloves, 32
coconut milk, 36
coconut rice, 51
cod, 24
see also salt cod
coffee, 35
coffee ice cream, 221
coffee mascarpone creams, 226
cookie dough, 42
cookies, 43

almond macaroons, 201
chocolate crispy cookies, 202
chocolate petit four cookies, 232
rich butter cookies, 200
cooking techniques, 14–15
coriander, 31
cumin- and coriander-rubbed
  lamb, 177
toasted coriander and cumin
  dressing, 45
coriander leaves, 29
coriander and spring onion
  rice, 51
crème fraîche and coriander
  chicken, 124
marinated smoked salmon with
  lime and, 182
roasted aubergines with feta
  and, 173
corn, 21
courgettes: marinated courgette
  and flageolet bean salad, 103
minty courgette linguine, 114
couscous, 40
cheesy leek and couscous
  cake, 119
grilled aubergine, mint and
  couscous salad, 102
crab, 25
Asian-style crab cakes, 121
crab and water chestnut
  wontons, 90
fresh crab sandwiches, 170
cranachan, 65
cranberry sauce, quick, 46
cream, 22
flavoured creams, 49
grilled pineapple and rum
  cream, 231
rhubarb and ginger trifles, 212
strawberry cream
  shortbreads, 213
crème fraîche: blinis with caviar
  and, 182
crème fraîche and coriander
  chicken, 124
croque monsieur, 72
Cuba libre, 242
cucumber: tomato and cucumber
  juice with basil, 236
cumin, 31
artichoke and cumin dip, 82
cumin- and coriander-rubbed
  lamb, 177
toasted coriander and cumin
  dressing, 45
curried cauliflower soup, 96
curried lamb samosas, 93
curry paste, 37
custard, 42
Portuguese custard tarts, 215
raspberry brûlée, 214

D
dairy produce, 22–3
deep-frying, 15
dill, 29
dips, 48
artichoke and cumin dip, 82
pepperonata, 82
dressings, 45
dried fruit, 36
drinks, 235–51
dry-frying, 14
spices, 15
duck, 27
marmalade and soy roast
  duck, 194

E
eggplant see aubergines
eggs, 23
creamy Parmesan baked
  eggs, 100
easy egg-fried rice, 50–1
eggs Benedict, 72
eggy bread panettone, 70
quick kedgeree, 75
seared tuna Niçoise, 100
see also omelettes
entertaining, 56, 181–97
equipment, 10–13

F
fennel: warm halloumi and fennel
  salad, 168
fennel seeds, 31
bocconcini with basil and, 184
figs, 19
baked apples with Marsala, 217
roast lamb with, 197
fish and shellfish, 24–5
flavouring, 16
stock, 44
see also individual types of fish
  and shellfish
flageolet beans: marinated
  courgette and flageolet bean
  salad, 103

flour, 38
flowers, edible, 35
focaccia, 53
with sardines and roast
  tomatoes, 104
fools, chocolate and banana, 210
fritters, salt cod and potato, 120
fromage frais: raspberry
  sherbet, 208
fruit, 18–19, 42
baby summer puddings, 222
summer berry frozen yogurt, 207
see also individual types of fruit
frying, 14–15

G
galangal, 33
game, 27
gammon, pan-fried with cider, 127
garam masala, 31
garlic, 33
aioli, 46
crushed new potatoes with basil
  and, 50
garlicky green salad with
  raspberry dressing, 150
pea soup with, 98
roast leg of lamb with rosemary
  and, 145
roast shoulder of lamb with
  whole garlic cloves, 144
rosemary and garlic
  marinade, 44
ginger, 32, 33
fragrant lemon grass and ginger
  pork patties, 126
ginger and soy marinade, 44
gingered carrot salad, 152
rhubarb and ginger trifles, 212
zingy papaya, lime and ginger
  salad, 62
gnocchi, home-made, 116
goose fat, crisp and golden
  roast potatoes with garlic
  and, 160
gooseberry relish, 46

NOTES

NOTES

NOTES

NOTES

NOTES

NOTES

NOTES

NOTES